NEIGHBORHOOD DEMOCRACY

NEIGHBORHOOD DEMOCRACY

A Model for Building Anchor Partnerships Between Colleges and Their Communities

Richard Guarasci

Foreword by Timothy K. Eatman

Published in Association with

Association of American Colleges and Universities

Routledge
Taylor & Francis Group

NEW YORK AND LONDON

First published 2022 by Stylus Publishing, LLC.
First Edition, 2022

Published 2023 by Routledge
605 Third Avenue, New York, NY 10017
4 Park Square, Milton Park, Abingdon, Oxon OX14 4RN

Routledge is an imprint of the Taylor & Francis Group, an informa business

© 2022 by Taylor & Francis

Library of Congress Cataloging-in-Publication Data
Names: Guarasci, Richard, author.
Title: Neighborhood democracy : a model for building anchor
    partnerships between colleges and their communities / Richard
    Guarasci ; foreword by Timothy K. Eatman.
Description: First Edition. | Sterling, Virginia : Stylus Publishing, LLC,
    [2022] | Includes bibliographical references and index. |
Identifiers: LCCN 2021050885
ISBN 9781642673562 (Cloth : acid-free paper) |
    ISBN 9781642673579 (Paperback : acid-free paper)

Subjects: LCSH: Democracy and education--United States. | Service
    learning--Study and teaching (Higher)--United States. | Civics--
    Study and teaching (Higher)--United States. | Community and
    college--United States. | Business and education--United States.
Classification: LCC LC89 .G83 2022 |
    DDC 378.1/03--dc23/eng/20220423
LC record available at https://lccn.loc.gov/2021050885

ISBN 13: 978-1-64267-357-9 (pbk)
ISBN 13: 978-1-64267-356-2 (hbk)
ISBN 13: 978-1-00-344613-2 (ebk)

DOI: 10.4324/9781003446132

*For my remarkable family, Carin, Bridget, Patrick,
Gaby, and Mani, and especially for
Zoe Amala Guarasci Potnuru, whose
bright light is a blessing to us all.*

CONTENTS

FOREWORD

Making my way to the Seaport restaurant where Richard and I meet for a long overdue dinner, I pause to note within me that exciting sense of anticipation familiar to anyone who reconnects with a true mentor and friend. When I arrive, he is already in place, having chosen an outside table with an awesome view of the riverscape and has almost finished converting our waiter to new friend—a natural effect of the warm Guarasci energy. The deceptively calm view of the city, including those two bodacious bridges that attempt to make peace among the almost always overly intense traffic flow between Manhattan and Brooklyn, as well as the distinctive skyline, proved a fitting and metaphorically gravid backdrop for our time together.

Early in the conversation he points to the approximate place in the East River where his grandfather harvested oysters in the early days after the Guarasci immigration to the United States from Italy. I appreciate very much how his communication is characteristically flavored with autobiography, an art that is an enduring feature of his parlance. While we do not talk much about the book specifically, its subject and message govern our conversation. As we catch up first on important family moments and then share reflections on the multiple pandemics—viral, racial, political, phenomenological—plaguing our world and higher education's potential for playing a role in its amelioration, I think over and over again about what an important sense of responsibility and discipline manifests in the pages that the reader will experience. Stories about his beloved Dr. Carin and granddaughter Zoe register with the same passion and caring interest as those of Esmeralda, Mindy, Tim, Nyema, Nick, and others in the book. The consonance of his treatment of family with the manner in which he shares the myriad stories in the book is authentic and striking, reflecting his holistic approach to living and education. I did not pass up the opportunity to snag some advice to nourish my own leadership and transformation projects. Seascape, bridges, river, traffic, harvest, oysters; dinner, a holistic life.

President Guarasci's documentation of leadership and learnings from his time at Wagner College does important work for higher education in general and the fields of publicly engaged scholarship and civic engagement in particular. I believe that at its core, this well-researched, rich, creatively crafted treatise provides a much-needed vision and corrective—*an unmasking of higher education, if you will.* In a time where mask use is prevalent and our society is acutely tuned in to the purpose of masks to protect each other from spreading viruses, we should not lose sight of the fact that masks can serve several both useful and not-so-useful functions. Among other things, they conceal, evoke imaginations, provide opportunities to expand fashion options, and in some cases promote a false sense of security. Sadly, masks have also become weaponized for political posturing and legal wrangling. Reading the manuscript provokes for me the unruly image of a huge, institution-sized mask with which the higher education community must reckon in order to realize its potential. As President Guarasci interrogates some of the traditional structures and practices of academe in the book, he calls for an *unmasking mandate.* He urges the higher education community to see how prophetic imagining, especially as it relates to rethinking relationships among higher education and shadow neighborhoods, can have a fortifying impact on our democracy.

Despite the fact that the story of my professional life is not possible without higher education, I have always been acutely aware of the aforementioned monster mask and its suffocating effects (Wilder, 2013). It is apparent in the ways we focus on students being college-ready rather than colleges being student-ready. The persistent, ubiquitous, and reliable gulf between secondary and postsecondary institutions of higher learning, especially for communities of color, evidence the mask. Policies and practices in academe, for example, that help maintain the status quo as it relates to lack of diversity among faculty; tenured faculty, to be sure, reveals a shrinking imagination that is well beneath the potential of 21st-century colleges and universities. Higher education as a sector cannot breathe if we refuse to take this unmasking mandate seriously. Like Richard, I am committed to revealing and interrogating this mask; it is challenging work, to say the least. His intentions for the book are emphatic:

> Higher education and American democracy require freedom of inquiry, informed citizens, and effective path ways for social and individual success. I will argue that the fate of both will depend on a major renewal of the civic mission of higher education in defense of a democracy that is socially inclusive, economically sustainable, and fundamentally just. (p. xv, this volume)

This is indeed an unmasking, but it is not inelegant. Richard reveals many of the entrenched dysfunctions and hurdles we face in academe with a balance of serious critique and imaginative purpose. To be sure, this firm but caring intervention interrogates the "ivory tower mindset" that I have written about elsewhere (Eatman et al., 2018)—that solipsistic celebration of being removed from community, which so profoundly mitigates the promise and verve of the 21st-century higher education enterprise. It also pivots on the evidentiary base about high-impact practices for student success (Kuh, 2008) placing special emphasis on one of my favorites, *service learning, community-based learning.* Importantly, the framework of full participation buttresses it all.

It is difficult to overstate the valuable impact of research on high-impact practices (HIPS) for student success, and yet in common practice it is honest to acknowledge that the efficacy of HIPS is too often diminished by the ivory tower mask. Research demonstrates that students who are traditionally underrepresented in higher education in general and students of color in particular tend to be underexposed to HIPS (McNair et al., 2020). This is true in spite of strong empirical evidence suggesting that HIPS can make a real positive difference in the educational experiences of these young people. It is only when HIPS are implemented within the framework of full participation that they can bear the ripest fruit. As Sturm et al. (2011) have noted, "Full participation is employed as a way of conceptualizing the intersections of student and faculty diversity, community engagement, and academic success as a nexus for the transformation of communities on and off campus" (p. 4). Guarasci's work with the Port Richmond Partnership Leadership Academy (PRPLA) embodies both the spirit and practice of Full Participation while deeply drawing on the principles of HIPS research. In his powerful book *Human Work*, Jamie Merisotis (2020) provides an expansive analysis of the relationship between college and career that pivots on the idea of broader knowledge skills (as opposed to the so often used framing of "soft skills"). Guarasci's book shows that civic education that employs HIPS and attends to the equity demands of Full Participation can facilitate a much needed sense of civic and citizenship responsibility to advance this democratic experiment to the next level.

Readers of this book will be compelled to consider the insights that Guarasci details to reflect upon and unmask their own work. That certainly is the case for me. There is a way in which this volume situates civic education as a dynamic dimension of Honors Education. Rutgers University-Newark, my home institution that Richard references among his exemplar institutions, is pursuing the civic imperatives of higher education, and espouses, claims, advances, and seeks to sustain an anchor institution philosophy and vision at a level I have not seen in my 30-year career in higher education. Under the leadership of Chancellor Nancy Cantor, who is truly Richard's comrade in arms, our institution takes seriously the necessary and urgent challenge to reimagine higher education in ways that are socially just and robust in its efforts to provide full participation to the communities it serves. Leaders like these acknowledge that while higher education has instigated significant movement toward equity and inclusion in the society as it has evolved, there is still so much more to be done. The Honors Living-Learning Community (HLLC) at Rutgers-Newark is one embodiment of that vision, an institutional transformation project rooted in the same ethos and vision as Wagner's PRPLA.

At its base, the HLLC is both a merit scholarship for room and board as well as a curriculum, carrying the requirements of a degree minor or second concentration in social justice. Through this work we are "revolutionizing, honors, cultivating talent and engaging communities" (Rutgers University-Newark, 2019, para. 2) with an acute emphasis on expanding opportunities and social capital for students who are traditionally underrepresented in higher education. This effort requires the operationalization of publicly engaged scholarship such that many if not most of the systems and processes within the university are rethought to understand the ways in which institutions have strategically disadvantaged many students, and doing so in ways that reflect an asset-based philosophy.

HLLC scholars, 50% of whom hail from the city of Newark, are highly aspiring students who in general have many higher education options and have chosen to spend their college years deeply engaged at an institution located within the community they love and believe can thrive. Indeed, it is not an overstatement to suggest that the HLLC, like PRPLA, bears all of the elements of a start-up. Unmasking the ivory tower requires this kind of thinking, planning, and bold action. From its novel two-phase interview process, which includes large- and small-group interviews conducted in partnership with a small army of campus and community-based partners who serve as evaluators to its multiple curricular pathways, the HLLC innovates in the higher education space with the goal of developing a national model.

The cohorts that result from the admissions process (since 2017) include 80 students, approximately two thirds of whom come directly from high school and one third who transfer from New Jersey community colleges and in some cases institutions at which students have completed the equivalent of 2 years of course work. Rutgers-Newark has seen an 80% increase in the enrollment of Newark residents in the last 8 years, and the HLLC plays a significant role in that change. It is critical that we identify, engage, and develop robust partnerships with community-based organizations to facilitate opportunities for meaningful experiential learning within the HLLC. High-touch student mentoring is at the core of our work. My team advances advising and mentoring systems grounded in regular one-to-one meetings with students to assist them in what I call scholar visioning. I share Chancellor Cantor's view that the HLLC is an innovation space for the larger campus. Its work is not possible without authentic and sophisticated relationships with community partners. The story of PRPLA bears this principle out with several compelling examples that Richard details in the book.

I resist the urge to detail further particulars about the HLLC admission process, institutional collaborations, courses, pathways, community partnerships, capstone, and brand new state-of-the-art multimillion dollar building. However, because of Richard's intellectual leadership and fulsome documentation of his Wagner journey, I am confident that readers will be inspired to reflect deeply on their own work. Richard would have us reflect in a way that looks beyond celebratory narratives rather to take up the trenchant charge to execute his unmasking mandate within the ivory tower. It is abundantly clear to me that institutional transformation projects on the order of PRPLA and HLLC—and I want to name College Unbound in Providence Rhode Island led by Dennis Littky and Adam Bush here—are located at the nexus of full participation and publicly engaged scholarship so that building democracy and creating partnerships can truly be leveraged toward the civic imperatives of higher education.

Earlier I noted that masks can evoke imaginations. The work of imagining (Boland et al., 2012) required to unmask the ivory tower is not light work. The reality is that higher education is responsible for much harm within communities as Baldwin's *In the Shadow of the Ivory Tower* (2021) reveals. Guarasci calls on us to rediscover neighborhood democracy believing as I do that this approach to college and university education can interrogate the abounding evidence of educational apartheid. One imagining that strikes me most powerfully in the book is Guarasci's *iron law of civic prosperity*—"good educational practice will increase net tuition revenue" (p. 58, this volume). No doubt, the reader will enjoy the story that he relays about sharing this principle with higher education leaders and business managers in a New York hotel. He courageously unpacks the economics of higher education in a nutshell. I am struck by his nuanced treatment of issues ranging from the scholarship of engagement to the "discount rate," complete with a sample budget table. This work of imagining proposes thought experiments and lays out practical examples, hypothetical models, illuminating statistics, and rich case studies as well as profiles in practice.

Most of all, this book reminds me afresh of how important it is to keep students at the center of our imagining, especially for those who have been traditionally underrepresented in higher education. They deserve our efforts to unmask the persisting myths and inequalities of higher education (Harris, 2021). As Richard recounted at dinner, we were not responsible about depleting the oyster population in the East River, but it is possible to bring the oysters back. The rivers of higher education present many possibilities for amelioration, but in each case they require that we cultivate a fuller understanding of how essential communities and community partners, primary and secondary schools, civic organizations, and the business community are to build bridges that create new pathways to redirect the overly intense flow of tradition that seems so difficult for higher education to surmount. Embracing "the arts of democracy," in Richard's words—which must always press toward liberatory education—may prove to be just the tool we need for unmasking higher education.

—Timothy K. Eatman
Dean of Honors Living-Learning Community,
and Associate Professor of Urban Education,
Rutgers-Newark

References

Baldwin, D. L. (2021). *In the shadow of the ivory tower: How universities are plundering our cities*. Bold Type Books.

Boland, K., Bott, K., Eatman, T., Haft, J., Peters, S., Ryerson, H., & Zahn, H. (2012). *What is the work of imagining*. Imagining America: Artists and Scholars in Public Life.

Eatman, T. K., Ivory, G., Saltmarsh, J., Middleton, M., Wittman, A., & Dolgon, C. (2018). Co-constructing knowledge spheres in the academy: Developing frameworks and tools for advancing publicly engaged scholarship. *Urban Education, 53*(4), 532–561. https://nls.ldls.org.uk/welcome.html?lsidyva2f31d27

Harris, A. (2021). *The state must provide: Why America's colleges have always been unequal—and how to set them right*. Ecco.

Kuh, G. D. (2008). *High-impact educational practices: What they are, who has access to them, and why they matter*. AAC&U.

McNair, T. B., Bensimon, E. M., Malcom-Piqueux, L. E., & Association of American Colleges and Universities. (2020). *From equity talk to equity walk: Expanding practitioner knowledge for racial justice in higher education*. Jossey-Bass.

Merisotis, J. P. (2020). *Human work: In the age of smart machines*. RosettaBooks.

Rutgers University-Newark. (2019). *Rutgers-Newark aligns with United Airlines to support students' travel for educational experiences*. Honors Living-Learning Community. https://hllc.newark.rutgers.edu/rutgers-newark-aligns-with-united-airlines-to-support-students-travel-for-educational-experiences/

Sturm, S., Eatman, T., Saltmarsh, J., & Bush, A. (2011). *Full participation: Building the architecture for diversity and public engagement in higher education* [White paper]. Columbia University Law School.

Wilder, C. S. (2013). *Ebony & ivy: Race, slavery, and the troubled history of America's universities*. Bloomsbury Press.

PREFACE

Higher education faces a civic imperative while American democracy is frail and in jeopardy. That both crises are occurring simultaneously is not an accident. Each is significantly dependent on the other. Finding a robust pathway to renewal for either one will demand a recognition that both are interrelated. Higher education and American democracy require freedom of inquiry, informed citizens, and effective pathways for social and individual success. In this book, I argue that the fate of both depends on a major renewal of the civic mission of higher education in defense of a democracy that is socially inclusive, economically sustainable, and fundamentally just.

American democracy suffers from an attack on its foundational values with the resurrection of two distinct pathologies, namely, the dramatic rise in social inequality and the resurgence of racism and ethnic subordination. Both jeopardize the soul of American democracy because the rising tide of inequality and racism threaten the essential public belief of the fairness of the democratic order. Without its legitimacy, democracies are more likely characterized by greater evidence of social decay, violent eruptions, and the disbelief in a better future.

From its origins, American higher education was expected to enhance democratic governance through the development of educated and responsible leaders and citizens who would be faithful to a free, fair, and orderly society. But just as American democracy needs higher education to reassert these civic responsibilities, colleges and universities find themselves trapped in a fiscal crisis that threatens their very institutional viability, the likes of which could easily lead them to abandon their commitments to democratic learning and civic engagement. And here is the rub. The fiscal crisis of higher education is, itself, rooted in the ascending social inequality and institutional racism that undermine democratic governance.

On this point, the breach of the American Constitution and its structure of democratic government threatens the foundations of free intellectual inquiry, the reliance on reason, objective evidence, and the rule of law. On January 6, 2021, the first insurrection against the federal government since the Civil War resulted in rioters storming the U.S. Capitol in an unmitigated attack on the joint session of Congress as it was certifying the electoral college vote of the legitimately elected forty-sixth president of the United States. This historic moment put to rest any false confidence that American democracy is impregnable and inevitable.

From the origins of the American republic, Benjamin Franklin and Thomas Jefferson argued that higher education has an obligation to prepare its students for their responsibilities as learned and engaged citizens. Universities accepted that challenge as part of the fabric of their existence. The civic mission of colleges has ebbed and waned during eras of economic, racial, and international strife, but now its civic role is paramount. Higher education must play an aggressive role in defending democracy. It cannot succeed and flourish without a vibrant commitment to an inclusive democracy that appreciates free inquiry with access and means for all who seek higher learning. In the face of explicitly antidemocratic political forces such as the rise of White supremacy, anti-intellectualism, nativist bias, and a "post truth" subculture, universities and colleges can no longer take sanctuary as civically disengaged and without public responsibility for the political health of American democracy.

But at this moment, the majority of colleges and universities are floundering under a business model that has resulted in insufficient net revenue while they are becoming less affordable. Too many of their students and their families are burdened with paralyzing educational debt. Moreover, these same institutions are confronted with stagnant or declining enrollments that, with their present business model, dramatically limit any sustainable pathways to fiscal stability. Finally, demographic realities project that the fastest and largest growing sectors in the United States are the minority communities, mostly Black and Brown, who possess the fewest financial resources to afford a college or university education.

The growing economic chasm between those who can afford higher education and those who cannot plays a dual role, undermining both American democracy and colleges and universities. Institutionalized racism and economic inequality result in persistent neighborhood segregation that serves as a dramatic barrier to an inclusive democracy and a vibrant economy. Economic inequality, coupled with institutionalized racism, erodes the civic fabric necessary for the legitimacy and success of a democratic system dependent upon a creditable narrative celebrating economic opportunity, individual liberty, and personal success.

The civic imperative of higher education is twofold. First, it must rebuild the knowledge and competency critical for a functioning, inclusive democracy and, as such, prepare its students to become responsibly engaged in sustaining a diverse society. Second, and most important, this project requires universities and colleges to build and prepare a new generation of students from poor Black and Brown neighborhoods that have been routinely neglected by, and subordinated to, a system of urban educational apartheid. Too many Black and Brown children are entrapped within what I will refer to as *shadow neighborhoods*—those that too often are invisible to the structures of power and privilege that surround them.

The purpose of this book is to chart a civic pathway for universities and colleges to renew their historic responsibility for rebuilding democracy through sustained partnerships with these shadow neighborhoods, becoming both allies and anchors with these communities as they rise together in symbiotic relationships framed around self-interest and mutual learning. This book is intended for all of the essential stakeholders of higher education, namely, presidents and chancellors, trustees and regents, faculty and staff, students and alumni. It also is meant as a charge for K–12 school leaders, major neighborhood nonprofit and corporate organizations, and public officials concerned about racial and economic justice. In short, it is aimed at the core constituencies that form strong university-neighborhood partnerships where each stakeholder group becomes an ally and anchor for the economic and civic prosperity of those invisible, shadow neighborhoods where those who are left out of the social mainstream of American life reside.

These anchor partnerships are not about altruism or a return of shadow communities as supplicants for university research and institutional needs. When based on equality, inclusion, and reciprocity, these partnerships are about building a deep commitment to democratic education, racial equity, and social transformation. They hold the potential for an expanded conception of a renewed American democracy where urban localism and citizen engagement balance out the personal estrangement and ensuing political passivity that too often can become the unintended impact of impersonal federal and state bureaucracies.

The fundamental argument of the book is presented in the first two chapters, Democracy in Peril and Universities in Crisis. Chapters 3 and 4 outline the historic and current civic mission of higher education. Chapter 5 makes the case for anchor partnerships as fiscally and educationally positive for higher education while serving as resource-rich pipelines for shadow neighborhoods. Chapter 6 offers a sampling of successful partnerships across the diverse tapestry of colleges, universities, and their neighborhoods.

Chapter 7 presents the human impact of civic work through a presentation of profiles of engaged high school and college students, faculty members, community partners, college administrators, and leaders. This was the most enjoyable chapter to write. Chapter 8 testifies to the economic and educational benefits of anchor partnerships for their local communities.

The last two chapters look toward resources and prospects for university-neighborhood partnerships. Chapter 9 outlines the roles, support, and opportunities available from the national higher education associations committed to this work. The final chapter explains the challenges and the promise of anchor partnerships for American democracy, higher education, and shadow neighborhoods. At the end of the book, I propose rediscovering "neighborhood democracy" as a viable approach to reinvigorating citizen participation and social transformation in building a new emerging generation of leaders for an inclusive, diverse, antiracist democratic order.

I have been rereading Ralph Ellison's enduring classic of American literature, *Invisible Man*. The concept of invisibility for the unnamed narrator remains even more prescient today. With the "new" visibility of the ever-present danger of institutionalized police violence against Black men and women and the rise of Black Lives Matter and its interracial allies, the United States has another opportunity to confront the deep scars of racism and bigotry. And, just as Ellison's central character, his unnamed narrator, must first make himself visible to himself and then to a greater White public, so, too, must all those who believe in the words of Amanda Gorman, youth poet laureate and presidential inaugural speaker, when she stated that in order to repair, all of us must become visible to one another: "Somehow we weathered and witnessed a nation that isn't broken but simply unfinished."[1] I believe that higher education can redeem its historic commitment to a vibrant and interracial American democracy through a sustained program of anchor partnerships with neighborhoods of need and a comprehensive educational dedication to civic learning and civic practice. The aim of this book is to demonstrate that civic imperative.

Notes

1. Camila Domonoske, "Not Broken, but Simply Unfinished," *NPR*, January 20, 2021, https://www.npr.org/sections/inauguration-day-live-updates/2021/01/20/958743170/poet-amanda-gorman-reads-the-hill-we-climb

ACKNOWLEDGMENTS

This book is the accumulation of many years of dedicated work for social reform in higher education. There are too many individuals to properly thank for their generosity and wisdom in shaping career-long efforts and movements that joined civic engagement and undergraduate learning. Regardless of program or institution, my goals always have been twofold, namely, to prepare students as engaged citizens and to involve higher education as an essential catalyst in creating a more inclusive, diverse, and equitable democracy in the United States.

I have many debts to pay to my colleagues at the national associations affiliated with civic engagement and social transformation. They include the Association of American Colleges and Universities, Campus Compact, the Coalition of Urban and Metropolitan Universities, the Anchor Institution Task Force, Project Pericles, and Bringing Theory to Practice.

My ideas and practice have benefited greatly over the years from my collaboration with faculty and administrative colleagues at St. Lawrence University, Hobart and William Smith Colleges, and Wagner College, all of whom provided support and intellectual challenges that helped me reflect and design my ideas and practice.

The most influential of these is my work at Wagner College in partnership with the Port Richmond community on Staten Island. The reader will encounter the depth of the Wagner College-Port Richmond Partnership in several of the chapters. As president of the college for seventeen years, I found a remarkable group of generative, resilient educators and community leaders who shaped the lives of children and young adults. Without the courage of Anthony Cosentino, Tim Gannon, Nick Mele, and Andrew Greenfield, there would be no educational pipeline for students who would have been overlooked. Instead, they earned scholarships and college degrees. They succeeded in high school, in part, because of an army of undergraduates, mostly Bonner scholars, as well as staff, including Arlette Cepeda, Kevin Farrell, Leo Schuchert, and Samantha Siegel, and faculty members Sarah Donovan, Rita Reynolds, Margarita Sanchez, and Lori Weintrob. Without these committed educators, these Port Richmond students would have faced the impact of the toxic mix of institutional racism, educational apartheid, and economic inequality.

The writing of this book was encouraged by Joe DeVitis and Chris Meyers. The work was carefully edited by the remarkable Amy Davis. Every word was read by Carin Guarasci. All the errors and omissions are mine. Additional assistance was provided by Paul Davidson, Ashley Finley, Patricia Fitzpatrick, Valerie Holton, and Bobbi Laur.

John von Knorring, Stylus Publishing, provided invaluable support and encouragement.

I

DEMOCRACY IN PERIL

Democracies are in peril throughout the world and no more so than in the United States. The rise of right-wing populism has resurrected the deep strain in American politics founded on nativism, ethnocentrism, anti-intellectualism, and, most deeply, naked racism and White supremacism. While always at play below the surface and spiking during eras of social change, economic stress, and international conflicts, the rise of what the late historian Richard Hofstadter named "the paranoid style of American politics" is now a paramount feature of the current scene. We are witness to a moment of remarkable social and political polarization with daily scenes of blatant bigotry on the one hand and bold displays of White supremacy on the other. In Charlottesville, Virginia, White supremacist groups marched with Nazi banners, chanting "Jews out," and in reference to Blacks, Browns, Asians, and others considered outside the heterosexual White race, they shouted, "You will not replace us." A few years later, we are witness to the murders of Black men and women by police authorities and others acting as White vigilantes, resulting in the largest street protests in the United States since the antiwar and civil rights protests of the 1960s. All of these events and so many more are part of a brazen attack on a diverse society and on the underlying principles of a democratic society.

These events are not isolated to the United States. Right-wing populism and antidemocratic movements are expanding across the globe. For instance, we are witnessing a wave of such developments in Eastern Europe, as exemplified in Hungary with the Jobbik Party under Viktor Orbán. A similar rise of influential parties is occurring in Slovakia with the Slovak National Party. Poland, too, is experiencing such nativist movements with the League for Polish Families. In Western Europe, Italy has seen the rise of The League under the leadership of Matteo Salvini, France with the growing efficacy of Marine Le Pen, and in Austria with its Freedom Party. Numerous other examples are spread across the European Union. In Latin America, the most

1

profound case is occurring in Brazil, led by Jair Bolsonaro. None of these movements are likely to disappear. All these parties cast themselves as replacements for the failure of liberal democracies to protect the relative privileges and legacies of entrenched ethnic and social interests.

In America, these efforts will not disappear with the absence of Donald Trump from public office. Nativist populism resides deeper within American political culture. At present, it is an attack on the legitimacy of constitutional government and the civic protocols that allow it to succeed. The aim of this movement is to ensure White racial privileges and political supremacy. As such, the American nativist impulse rests on a psychological foundation based on the fears of social replacement and declining economic significance.

Two Fates

On a recent sunny Staten Island day, a petite Latina graduate moved to the microphone at her Port Richmond High School (PRHS) commencement. As she approached the podium, a distinct feeling of tension was in the air. Esmeralda is a somewhat shy and quiet Mexican young woman. She comes from one of the many Oaxaca families that migrated to New York City's smallest borough.

The event was held at Wagner College's gymnasium, two miles from the high school. The audience was a mix of Mexican, Mexican American, African American, and White working-class families. Port Richmond is a neighborhood of approximately 11,000 residents in a borough of nearly 500,000 residents within a city of eight and a half million New Yorkers. Port Richmond is clearly marked as a poor, struggling community with a history of ethnic and racial conflict. The cultural and ethnic differences are especially pronounced for the Mexican community. Most members of the community, which is composed of hardworking multigenerational new immigrant families, live in the shadows, fearful of authority and seeking safety in their churches and through strong family bonds. They are refugees from the violence and poverty of rural Mexico. Many fled with nothing except what they could carry, landing in a highly diverse New York City.

I was privileged to be on the commencement stage, along with other local and school leaders. Reflective of the community, the audience was animated and capable of both affirmative and explosive public outbursts. I was fearful for Esmeralda. I wanted her to rise to the moment. Her shyness prompted my instincts to be protective of her and many of her classmates whom I had come to admire for their deep desire to break through the barriers of the social forces that suppress the talents of poor inner-city boys and girls.

My stress rose with Esmeralda's opening line: "I am going to share a secret with you today that I have never told to anyone else." These are dangerous words in a neighborhood rich with undocumented residents as well as too many who are intolerant of social differences outside the traditional mainstream and oppositional political views. I didn't know where she was going with this. Was this about to become an autobiographical confession that would easily test the tolerance of this mixed audience? Naturally, my apprehension grew with the suspense of awaiting her next words.

"I love math. I love math because math is the same in Colombia and Mexico as it is in Asia, Europe, and even on Staten Island." Wow! Esmeralda went on to draw out her argument and this amazing metaphor for human connection in an age filled with anti-immigrant, racial, gender, and religious bigotry, which her family witnesses almost daily through exclusions on the street, in the workplace, or in the schools. I was stunned by her brilliance and her thoughtful idealism. She never formally mentioned race, ethnicity, or gender in her speech. It wasn't necessary. The elegance of the metaphor spoke to its insight and wisdom.

In her quiet and reserved manner, Esmeralda painted many pictures with the power and meaning of her words. She captured the deep thirst for learning that is usually washed out in impoverished schools and violent neighborhoods. She wants to see the world as wide and deep. She has boundless curiosity about opportunities she can't easily access, and she has a deep desire to discover her ethnic and familial legacies. She captured her creativity and intellectual capacity, which is shared by so many of her classmates but usually stunted by frail and underresourced learning environments, economic barriers, violence and trauma, and, most centrally, a school system trapped in de facto educational apartheid.

Esmeralda's words spoke to the light of a better future, to a world of fairness, personal achievement, and open possibilities. It would also be a world of social tolerance where everyone is treated with the same opportunities— where math is the same as it is on Staten Island. I left that commencement with so much hope about the possibilities for educating and nurturing a new generation of truly transformative leaders capable of designing, building, and sustaining an inclusive democracy and a dynamic economy.

Four years later, Esmeralda is a graduate of Baruch College of The City University of New York (CUNY). She was part of a successful alliance between PRHS and Wagner College, the leading institutions in the larger Port Richmond Partnership Leadership Academy (PRPLA), which engages college readiness, health inequalities, immigration justice, economic development, the arts, and public history.[1] In cohorts of twelve high school students per class year, freshman PRHS students apply for acceptance into a college preparatory program with Wagner where they take three years of courses, coupled with field-based civic engagement in their own community. Their college courses are taught by full-time Wagner College faculty, and upon completion of the PRPLA program, each student earns a full semester of college credits—before they enter college. They also reside on campus in the summers.

The goal of the PRPLA is to prepare students to succeed not only in high school but also in college and go on to become engaged leaders in their careers and communities. The program was intentionally aimed at students with high school averages of 75 to 82 after their first year of high school, based on the belief that students performing above this level would persist in their education and earn a high school degree and would be attractive candidates for college admission. Esmeralda and her eleven PRPLA colleagues were accepted into universities and received significant, if not total, financial support.

One of Esmeralda's student colleagues, Mindy, is another example of the power these types of neighborhood partnerships hold for youngsters who receive daily messages about their inadequacies and destinies preordained by their economic circumstances. Mindy is a very smart Latina, a present and engaged natural leader. You spot her immediately as having unlimited potential. She also was surrounded by gangs and their promise of easy opportunities that surely would result in abandoning high school. PRPLA recruited her as a high school freshman. She resisted mightily, saying the program was "not her thing." With the insistence of her remarkable high school principal, Mindy joined the program. Every day was a struggle. "It's too hard. I am not college material," she said.

Mindy made it through PRHS and then into Wagner College. She wanted to be a nurse. I would tell her that she had the capacity to excel as a health professional and my expectation was that she would be leading a hospital staff someday, bringing her commitment to ending health disparities and helping so many others along the way. Again, every semester was a challenge. "It's too hard," Mindy said. "I am not that smart."

With the insistence of her teachers, her nursing dean, and many others, Mindy is now on her way to a successful nursing career.

Mindy and Esmeralda are but two examples of the power that university and K–12 partnerships can achieve. They can change lives in dramatic ways and, even more importantly, can prepare a generation of diverse transformational leaders who are capable of rescuing our democracy from its current blight of bigotry, division, and decline. A number of universities and colleges are now creating a deliberate movement to form similar partnerships with local schools in distressed neighboring communities. Often these school partnerships are part of a larger set of commitments that bridge into other areas suffering from racial, ethnic, and class inequalities, such as inadequate health care, discriminatory criminal justice, environmental crises, justice for new immigrants, the lack of economic development, and suppressed political participation. All of these areas are represented in university curriculums, research programs, and professional preparation. Consequently, higher education retains a good physical and social capital that can be aligned with shadow communities in nearby settings. We see this work emerging at a significant number of institutions, large and small, public and private. This landscape includes such nationally renowned institutions as the University of Pennsylvania and Johns Hopkins University; regional comprehensives like Rutgers University campuses in Newark and Camden, the University of Nebraska in Omaha, and Drexel University in Philadelphia; and small private colleges such as Augsburg University in Minneapolis and Wagner College in New York City on Staten Island.

If higher education is to become, as it should, one of the vital social agencies attacking the plight of class and racial/ethnic inequality, it must first rediscover its own individual founding missions where advancing social mobility and building a vibrant democracy are fundamental to its own legacy, essential to its civic responsibility, and, I would argue, critical to its own fiscal stability. Neighborhood partnerships like the one that found Esmeralda and then committed to her and her fellow students are one powerful pathway for colleges and universities to assert this civic role.

The experiences of Esmeralda and Mindy are unusual if not unique. The all-too-familiar narrative is one of predominantly Black and Brown children lost and ultimately abandoned in shadow neighborhoods strewn throughout urban and metropolitan America. They are caught in an urban swirl of poverty, class, race, and ethnicity that circumscribes neighborhoods fraught with failing and underfunded schools, high levels of violence and personal trauma, and significantly higher levels of hypertension, heart disease, diabetes, strokes, and cancers—all leading to lower life expectancy and much higher rates of joblessness and underemployment. Here, life adjusts to lower expectations, both those imposed by outsiders and those habituated from insiders.

To visualize this context, I can think of no more impactful example than that drawn out in Wes Moore's brilliant memoir of growing up in Baltimore, *The Other Wes Moore.*[2] In this remarkable story of two young boys growing up in the same city, a few blocks from each other, with the exact same name, one ends up as a university graduate, decorated veteran, White House Fellow, and Rhodes Scholar while the other sits in prison with a lifetime sentence for homicide, robbed of a life of meaning and impact. What caused such disparate life outcomes for two young boys with so much in common? How does one explain it? Is it coincidence, destiny, character, or guidance and mentorship? Both young lives were painted by gangs, recurrent neighborhood violence, illegal drugs, pervasive racial segregation, and dispossession by the larger political and governmental apparatus. The answer may reside not in luck but in the residue of intervention, resilience, and partnership.

In the early 1990s, the Baltimore City Public Schools maintained a high school graduation rate below 40 percent while the rate in the surrounding Baltimore County area, which was more economically secure, was in the mid-80 percent range. Opportunity is dispersed and defined by race and class. In a thirty-year study of Baltimore's inner-city children and their life success, Karl Alexander and his colleagues found that only 4 percent of the initial 790 inner-city poor children they studied through their adulthood attained a college degree compared with the larger population rate of 45 percent.[3] They summed up their findings with examples of what they termed "haunted stories of young men in jail . . . who, on the path to adulthood, neighborhood, family, and school conspire to pass down advantage and disadvantages from generation to generation."

When looking deeper into race, poverty, and educational outcomes, journalist Tanvi Misra found some startling statistics.[4] In generally low-income and racially segregated neighborhoods, schools were underfunded and maintained significantly lower resources and educational opportunities, all leading to lower performance. The U.S. government defines poor schools as those that have a majority of students qualifying for free or heavily subsidized school lunches. Misra's research found that poor, particularly Black and Brown, students are six times more likely to attend poor and low-performing schools. She goes on to state that in Chicago, 75 percent of Black teenagers attend high-poverty schools while only 10 percent of White students do so. These patterns are evidence of profound consequences of the realities of inner-city racial and class discrimination and neglect, which I would characterize as painting the outer veneer of America's urban educational de facto apartheid. In fact, New York City's public school system is now more segregated than it was at the time of the U.S. Supreme Court's landmark 1954 decision in *Brown v. the Board of Education*. The decision ended the legal segregation sanctioned by the court's 1896 judgment in *Plessy v. Ferguson*, which upheld the "separate but equal" ruling of the lower courts.

Scholar Pedro Noguera and his colleagues have conducted extensive research on urban schools, and they found five key characteristics of these institutions.[5] These schools manifest persistently low student achievement; they lack instructional coherence; they maintain inexperienced teaching staff due to teacher turnover and attrition; they have poorly functioning business and data systems resulting in an inability to trace issues and trends; and they persist with low expectations of their students. This work shows us how systems of race, ethnicity, and class are sustained as "self-fulfilling prophecies."

Americans like to cling to the belief that individual merit determines life chances. We reject any fatalistic determinism that class and race preset the outcomes for poor children. When we encounter some of the previously outlined data, that position becomes more untenable. There is always a ladder to the middle class by working hard and succeeding against the odds. But just as one reaches for that comfortable position, we encounter Michelle Bassetti's research on urban educational funding disparities.[6] She finds that not only are there significant funding disparities per child in different school districts, but the state of infrastructure becomes an additional barrier to educational outcomes. In Camden, New Jersey, schools spend $1,500 per child with a resulting 48 percent high school graduation rate. Camden schools are 100 percent minority students. In the adjacent and more advantaged Collingswood, New Jersey, a borough of Camden, educational spending is $7,500 per student, with a 47 percent minority enrollment and a high school graduation rate of 94 percent. This disparity presents a vivid illustration of social and economic inequalities, side by side, in the same state and within the same metropolitan space.

In reality, American schools are part of a "myth of meritocracy" where those children educated in schools and communities that provide substantial resources can rise or fall based on their hard work and natural abilities, while in distressed neighborhoods with shadow schools, the children find themselves engulfed in segregated systems with few opportunities for advancement and school success. Here, the extraordinary few, usually accompanied by a family advocate and an exceptional teacher or mentor, find a way to overcome these barriers. The remainder sink before they even have a reasonable chance to succeed, drowning early because of inadequate reading competency, or a short time later because they lack the math skills that would allow them to be placed in algebra classes, the ticket to a college preparatory high school track.

Americans reject social and economic determinism, but the previously cited statistics make that state of denial more difficult to maintain. Here are more troubling statistics. In the United States, students who are not on the third-grade reading level by the start of the fourth grade are unlikely to graduate high school. In fact, these students constitute 63 percent of all high school dropouts.[7] Among fourth-grade students, 74 percent who demonstrate the lowest levels of reading proficiency are from low-income families. The situation is actually worse because 50 percent of Black and

47 percent of Latino students have below-basic reading skills. These statistics allow us to understand why low-income students are thirteen times less likely to graduate high school than their peers from other income groups. Moreover, poor reading proficiency correlates with prison incarceration, because 70 percent of all prison inmates in the United States read at the fourth-grade level or below.

In short, reading profoundly shapes destiny, and reading is influenced by the effectiveness of schools, the dynamics of race and class in inner-city neighborhoods, and families submerged in an urban stew of poverty, racism, and violence. How does any type of democracy survive this? And what responsibility do universities and colleges have to become allies and partners in assisting schools and neighborhoods in reversing this calamity? How do we stop ending up with two Wes Moores instead of a generation of just the successful and productive one? As Richard Milner brilliantly observes in *Rac(e)ing to Class*, as so many Black and Brown inner-city students work through continuing encounters with violence and death, how do we prepare teachers to understand the trauma as a form of posttraumatic stress disorder?[8] How do we support these children in the early grades so their initial instinct to learn does not fade in the wake of battle-like syndromes?

The New and Divided City

As stark as these realities may be, they have been with us for some time. They persist with a resilience that appears insurmountable to even the most optimistic urban planners and city mayors. We are now in the midst of persistent intergenerational poverty. According to Allan Mallach, among others, we are witness to a regenerative rate of racial and class inequality that is becoming acute in major American cities.[9] Since the turn of the century, this trend has expanded at an alarming rate. For instance, the widening income gap in Baltimore has grown significantly since 2000. That year, Black family median income was 61 percent of White median income. By 2015, this percentage dropped to 48 percent. Richard Florida, the noted American urban analyst, notes that between 1979 and 2007, the top 1 percent of income earners gained 53 percent of the overall increase in income, but by 2013 the inequality gap jumped significantly.[10] The top 1 percent of income earners were making 25 times the average income of the remaining 99 percent. In New York City, the top 1 percent were making 40 times the income of the remaining 99 percent. Both income inequality and wage inequality were driving the dangerous gaps between the super-rich, the well-off, the working class, and those at the bottom.

When we couple income and wealth gaps with a resurgent urban racial segregation, we gain a better understanding of the macroeconomic underpinnings of the segregated, underresourced, and failing schools in inner-city, impoverished neighborhoods. Add an unresponsive, if not gerrymandered, political system, and we expose the fabric of the current urban political economy. It frames a harsh, if not brutal, sociology and urban geography for Black, Brown, and poor residents. The ladders to escape from a fate of intergenerational poverty are absent all but a few rungs. Social determinism crafts an urban and racial fatalism for the Black and Brown underclass, trapped in urban neighborhoods seemingly designed to incarcerate them in or out of formal prisons.

Mallach argues that more jobs by themselves are not the antidote. They may become traps in and of themselves. With low pay, few or no benefits, and significantly limited chances for social mobility, too many of these bottom-end jobs merely keep the cycle of impoverishment and immobility in place. In the current economy, a clear divide exists between those educated with twenty-first-century job skills and those left without them. Although technological skills are part of the necessary competencies, they are not the only ones needed. The current and emerging economy requires effective communication skills, problem-solving ability, critical thinking capacity, creativity, and collaborative habits. This economy requires competence in many of the so-called soft skills that revolve around social and emotional development as well as civic capacities. To break the cycle of poverty and significantly reduce economic and racial inequality, K–12 schools in shadow neighborhoods must drastically improve. They have been unable to break through with the traditional array of K–12 stakeholders, namely boards of education, political leaders, teacher unions, public and charter schools, and policymakers. They desperately need new and highly committed allies.

Colleges and universities can be part of a new coalition allied with employers, local governments, and philanthropy. Doing so is imperative. First, those who attain four-year college degrees earn over 70 percent more than those without, compared with 52 percent in 1997. The new economy is vastly increasing the income and poverty gap. In fact, Richard Florida argues there is a new urban crisis where the factors that are responsible for urban economic growth are simultaneously driving greater levels of inequality. Residential segregation, gentrification, and educational gaps are driving the middle class out of these cities while also deeply imprisoning the poor in declining and forgotten neighborhoods. At the same time, these cities are giving birth to islands of urban affluence that disproportionately benefit from the same dynamics at an exponential rate.

The incidence of the two Wes Moores may be remembered as a quaint reality in another generation or two when we only have one version of Wes Moore, the one sitting in prison with a lifetime sentence.

Moving Forward

Two fates: Esmeralda and Mindy on one side or on the other Wes Moore, incarcerated in prison, already a grandfather and with little hope of having much in the way of a personal and intimate relationship with the next generation of Moores. Yet Esmeralda and Mindy and many like them who are benefiting from university and college neighborhood partnerships are a hopeful pathway to a better personal life. They hold out the possibility of breaking the cycle. They possess the skills of civic professionals and community leaders who could underscore the hope of a better, more inclusive, equitable, and dynamic political economy.

The intentional collaboration of what we call anchor partnerships, each partner anchored in each other's life for mutual benefit, can become a beacon of a different future for both shadow neighborhoods and for universities and colleges. They each can build higher expectations for one another. As the imprisoned Wes Moore says to the successful one when asked why it turned out so differently for each of them, "maybe (we are) products of our expectations. . . . I mean others' expectations that you take on as your own."

Anchor partners develop these expectations of each other. These neighborhoods need allies with physical and social capital to listen, learn, teach, mentor, believe, and fight with and for them. Colleges and universities desperately need to rediscover their civic mission and reestablish themselves as public providers of a public good, not simply for private advancement. They also must prepare future generations of college-ready students, particularly from the fastest growing parts of the American population, if they are to have the numbers to fill their seats. Together, universities and shadow neighborhoods can become—and in some places are becoming—anchors and allies for one another and for a better and sustainable future.

The civic imperative compels both to act. In later chapters, we will discuss many examples of promising practice. The work is underway. Whether these anchor partnerships can sustain themselves and overcome their own internal and external barriers will determine their impact on racial and class inequality. To be sure, the most important element in their success must be the education and preparation of transformational and engaged democratic future leaders, capable and ready to nurture a more inclusive politics and a more dynamic economy.

Notes

1. The Port Richmond Partnership Leadership Academy (PRPLA) was generously supported by grants and gifts from The New World Foundation, The Charles Hayden Foundation, The Richmond County Bank Savings Foundation, The Northfield Bank Foundation, and by Patrick and Marion Dugan.

2. Wes Moore, *The Other Wes Moore: One Name, Two Fates* (New York: Random House, 2010).

3. Karl Alexander, Doris Entwisle, and Linda Olson, *The Long Shadow: Family Background, Disadvantaged Urban Youth, and the Transition to Adulthood* (New York: Russell Sage Foundation, 2014), 5.

4. Tanvi Misra, "The Stark Inequality of U.S. Public Schools, Mapped," *Bloomberg*, May 14, 2015, CityLab, www.citylab.com.

5. Pedro Noguera, Roey Ahram, Adeyemi Stembridge, and Edward Fergus, "Framing Urban School Challenges: The Problems to Examine When Implementing Response to Intervention," *RTI Action Newsletter*, 2011, http://rtinetwork.org/component/content/article/12/465-framing-urban-school

6. Michelle Bassetti, "Academic Inequality in the Urban School Setting: Funding Disparities That Lead to Educational Disadvantages," *PA Times*, February 9, 2018, www.patimes.org.

7. Data on income and literacy can be found in "Early Warning Confirmed: A Research Update on Third Grade Reading," Annie E. Casey Foundation, November 3, 2013; on race and literacy in Sarah E. Redfield and Jason Nance, "School to Prison Pipeline: Preliminary Report," American Bar Association, February 2016; on income and graduation in John Hudson, "An Urban Myth That Should Be True," *The Atlantic*, July 12, 2012; on impact on early childhood experiences in Donald J. Hernandez, "Double Jeopardy: How Third Grade Reading Skills and Poverty Influence High School Graduation," Annie E. Casey Foundation, April 2011.

8. H. Richard Milner IV, *Rac(e)ing to Class: Confronting Poverty and Race in Schools and Classrooms* (Cambridge, MA: Harvard University Press, 2017).

9. Alan Mallach, *The Divided City: Poverty and Prosperity in Urban America* (Washington DC: Island Press, 2018).

10. Richard Florida, *The New Urban Crisis* (New York: Basic Books, 2018).

2

UNIVERSITIES IN CRISIS

American universities are in dire distress. While the few universities that are heavily endowed remain stable, many others fear for their own survival. A number of institutions already have failed and no longer exist. Most believe they can escape a fiscal catastrophe, but they work under conditions of significant uncertainty. Since 2016, a national higher education watchdog has tracked sixty universities and colleges that have closed or merged in twenty-six states.[1]

A number of factors contribute to the vulnerability of universities and colleges. They suffer from fiscal challenges around pricing, affordability, and student debt, which results in inadequate revenues to sustain their institutional stability. Most universities and colleges depend on tuition for 90 percent or more of their operating revenue, which means student enrollment is the critical source of their revenue. Student enrollment, however, is stagnating. Similarly troubling for these institutions, the fastest growing portion of the American population is among those families least able to afford college. If these individuals are going to enroll and complete their degrees, they are likely to require lower tuition and more financial assistance.

These factors, alone, would seem sufficient for causing a financial tsunami for higher education, but additional challenges surround campuses. The public's appreciation of the college degree may be in decline, and the public trust of higher education is definitely falling.[2] Everything from the perceived escalating cost of college to scandals in admissions, athletics, and, in some cases, exorbitant executive compensation, combine for a decline in the favorability ratings of universities and colleges.

Higher education is facing its greatest challenges since the Great Depression, and in many ways, they are even more difficult to overcome than those in the 1930s. Then, only a distinct minority, less than a third of those eligible, attended college. For the most part, a college education was the domain of the privileged. In contrast, a college degree is now a necessity for almost everyone seeking economic security.

The escalation of economic inequality, which is tied closely to racial inequity, illuminates the dilemmas of shadow neighborhoods and colleges and universities while revealing their interrelationships. In an age of omnipresent technological innovation, the American economy needs a college-educated workforce. Those outside the technological divide are left to low-paying, benefit-absent service jobs without much in the way of income stability. At the same time, colleges and universities require a large percentage of the population to attend their institutions and yet the prospects for that outcome are becoming more elusive.

In short, higher education needs to attend to the educational success of more students from underserved neighborhoods while these neighborhoods desperately need new allies and partners to break through the barriers of inequality. Anchors need allies, and allies can become anchors for one another through a renewed civic commitment to an inclusive democracy. This chapter will outline the crisis of universities and introduce the promise of higher education's civic mission as a possible pathway to its financial stability and public responsibility.

The Fiscal Crisis of Higher Education

Understanding the economics of higher education can be a trying exercise for those outside the academy. In my experience as a longtime college president, even sophisticated university trustees with advanced careers in business found the entire fiscal structure of universities mysterious if not oxymoronic. This shouldn't be so because it is basically a simple enterprise. The confusion comes from higher education's economic structure or what is better described as its "business model."

For the large majority of campuses, the enterprise is fairly simple to comprehend once it is reduced to the basic elements of revenue and expense. First, campus revenue comes largely from student tuition. For those colleges and universities offering residence and dining services, these functions provide additional revenue. Endowments, the major investment funds of colleges and universities, can add additional revenue from earnings as these funds increase. They are usually expected to provide no more than 5 percent from the corpus of the investment fund on average. Of course, these investments are subject to the markets and the success of asset allocation decisions, which means they can decline as well as increase in any given period.

Many institutions have additional sources of revenue depending on their size and scope. Large research universities have sizable research facilities, which depend on competitive grants as well as gifts to cover operations. Those institutions in major college athletics, particularly with highly televised NCAA Division I football and basketball programs, will realize significant revenue funds. Smaller institutions may experience modest athletics revenue, although it is generally inadequate in meeting operating expenses.

Many institutions have development revenue generated from annual and planned giving operations as well as major contributions to capital campaigns. Most colleges have a myriad of less significant sources of revenue such as college stores, the provision of contracted services, and other smaller items. These constitute the majority of revenue items. Universities with medical centers and other entrepreneurial enterprises can have other major revenue sources. Some of these are attached to professional schools in law, the applied sciences, and education, among others.

However, expenses are similarly simple for most institutions. Personnel is an exceptionally large expense, which includes compensation and benefits as the major items. The institutions employ faculty members, administrators, support staff, maintenance and grounds personnel, public safety officers, medical and counseling staff, athletics coaches and administrators, residence hall staff, business and finance staff, human relations specialists, fundraising staff, information technology specialists, and other staff. Personnel expenses often account for more than half the operating budget—even greater if we include large medical, research, and laboratory staffs.

Operating and maintaining buildings and campus grounds is expensive. Marketing and recruiting students are sizable expenditures. Communications and institutional promotion add expense. And, of course, dining, health services, and other related expenses add up. The elephant in the room for most colleges and universities, however, is the significant expense of supporting students through the institution's own financial aid assistance. This factor has grown exponentially in the past twenty-five-plus years. It does not include any outside scholarships and awards such as government grants, loans, or scholarships provided by outside organizations. Those are noninstitutional funds. College and university financial aid reduces student tuition by the financial aid amount allocated. Consequently, it is commonly referred to as the "tuition discount," similar to a price discount in an ordinary retail purchase. The percentage discounted is known as the discount rate.

In the past twenty-five years or so, the discount rate has grown enormously. It is fast becoming the largest expense item. According to a recent study, the discount rate for all undergraduates rose from 34.7 percent in 2007 to 46.3 percent by 2018. For first-year students over the same time period, the discount rate increased from 39 percent to 52.2 percent.[3] In previous eras, institutions would offer prospective students institutional financial aid based on the demonstrated financial family need. In the past thirty years, private colleges and universities introduced merit scholarships as well as need-based scholarships. From my own experience and observations, these institutions were anxious about losing the middle and the upper-middle classes to the lower-priced public universities. To recapture some of this enrollment, the privates augmented their growing financial aid budgets with these merit scholarships. The result was an ever-escalating discount rate, as the privates not only competed with public institutions but also tried to match their rival institutions.

More recently, public universities have introduced tuition discounting into their admissions programs. In my career as a senior administrator from 1992 until the end of my presidency in 2019, I watched the discount rate of small northeastern colleges rise from 20 percent to more than 50 percent. Some colleges fighting for survival are discounting more than 70 percent, which means they garner a net tuition of 30 cents on the dollar from their tuition rates. This cycle of discounting competition is only getting worse.

As competition for enrollment has increased and the discount business model has become standing practice, the impact on revenue is severe. Tuition minus the institutional financial aid is the net or actual tuition dollars collected by the university. With the expansion of the discount business model in the past two decades, the actual net tuition revenue is largely flat. While the advertised tuition prices ("sticker prices") have increased significantly in this period—and quite significantly among private colleges—these institutions are garnering approximately the same amount of net tuition per student. From 1987 to 2017, private colleges increased the sticker price by 213 percent and public institutions by 129 percent; however, net tuition per student has increased modestly.[4] It slowed considerably after the recession of 2008. In other words, tuition sticker prices have increased, but the actual average price paid is somewhat static.

The consumer market for higher education has de facto repriced the college degree in part because the ability to pay has barely grown. Real median family income was actually close to zero during this period. In addition, the discount wars among colleges and universities have encountered real bargaining by families as they seek ever lower net or actual costs to attend. The cohort of families unwilling to pay is as significant as the group experiencing an inability to pay the asking price. Finally, the growth of income and wealth disparities, particularly in the bottom 20 percent, has made college and degree completion an even more distant dream for students and families of color in shadow neighborhoods.

The upshot of the discount business model is that higher education institutions suffer genuine fiscal stress. Their costs increase for all the previously listed expense items, while their revenue is virtually flat. Couple this fiscal crisis with the explosion of student loan debt in the past twenty years, and colleges encounter another major challenge, namely affordability. Between 1999 and 2015, the percentage of students incurring loans for college increased from 49 percent to 71 percent.[5] In the same period, the amount of accumulated debt per student rose from approximately $17,000 to approximately $30,000. It is now more than $35,000. These statistics apply to those graduating but do not account for those who do not complete the degree.

Approximately 37 percent of those students taking loans do not complete either an associate or bachelor's degree and they are behind on their payments.[6] These are students who borrowed to acquire a degree with the expectation of increasing their annual income and financial stability, only to fail in that pursuit. What they did acquire was a significantly worse financial situation, burdened with debt, for which federal law prevents them from accessing federal bankruptcy relief. Too often, these are residents of shadow neighborhoods.

All of this fiscal stress on colleges, universities, students, and families is a result of a dysfunctional business model for financing higher education. The discount wars have led to the creation of a bubble for higher education institutions where the "tragedy of the commons" overwhelms institutional decision-making. Each individual institution fears being the outlier that bucks the system, refusing to compete on scholarship discounting. The college would be overwhelmed by its competitors and would fear suffering a large enrollment decrease, and, of course, a major loss of net revenue. The majority of colleges recoil at ending the discount practice. To cease competing with other colleges in this way is risky, yet college leadership has no facile answer to replace it.

For instance, by significantly reducing price and the accompanying financial aid, a "price reset," colleges and universities would have to increase their attractiveness to prospective students to offset the lower tuition with a sizable enrollment increase. If that fails and there is less tuition revenue, colleges are exposed to actual revenue decline. Two institutions with which I am familiar tried price resetting, and in both cases net revenue declined. In the end, consumers perceive the price reduction experiment as an act of desperation. In general, today's institutions want to avoid the perception that they pose a risk to potential students, donors, investors, and competitors.

Without a significant increase in student enrollment, the key source of their revenue, most colleges and universities are facing a punishing future.

Typically, they try to manage this through austerity, but that only makes them less attractive to potential students in the long run. Cutting expenses ultimately means cutting staff, faculty, and programs that in and of themselves may reduce net revenue. The alternatives to austerity are limited, but the most popular is the addition of programs to increase tuition revenue. This is another risk because upfront, added programs often require further investments in personnel, space, materials, and, ironically, more institutional financial aid. If these new initiatives fail to yield significant enrollment, they add to the fiscal deficit.

The Loss of the Public Trust

The Pew Research Center has been tracking public perceptions of higher education for some time. The current results of their surveys are troubling for colleges and universities. While there is a public recognition of the economic benefits of a college degree, associate or bachelor's, there is a growing suspicion of higher education and its practices. Given the hyper-partisanship within the current public domain, much of this negativity falls along political party identification.[7] Beyond the political divide, there is evidence of the public's weariness of a number of self-inflicted wounds by colleges and universities, including the escalating tuition pricing, the growing fear of student debt, the incidence of scandals in admissions and athletics, and overcompensation. There is some evidence of the distrust of indoctrination and the limiting of free speech on campus, but this falls along partisan lines for the most part. In sum, all of these issues lead to a significant challenge for colleges and universities in regaining the public trust and in restoring faith in higher education.

In the Pew Research survey, a majority of the respondents affirmed that they believed higher education was generally heading in the wrong direction. Those identifying as Democrats were less sure of this (52 percent), but those identifying as Republicans concurred by a very large majority (73 percent). By far, both sides strongly identified excessive tuition costs as the main problem (84 percent). A smaller, but significant, majority felt that students were not acquiring the skills necessary to succeed in the workplace (65 percent). They generally were split on concerns about political indoctrination by professors or repression of views students may find offensive, although those identifying as Republicans were more troubled by these latter points.

The Pew survey questions the fairness of the admissions process. One can only speculate, but it is reasonable to infer from current admissions scandals and subsequent prosecutions that this public concern has increased since the 2017 survey. However, this survey shows significant public support for ensuring that colleges are representative of races and cultures and that they maintain ethnically and racially diverse student enrollment.

Despite all of these findings, there is public recognition that a college degree is important, if not essential. It is not the only important variable. Survey respondents also cite the importance of a strong work ethic, the ability to collaborate with fellow employees, and the acquisition of the appropriate job skills. Later in this book, I will provide some interesting survey data on what chief operating officers of large and small employers seek in college graduates. Surprisingly, the findings affirm many of the academic and social skills that are introduced in college. The specific experiences gained from student involvement in civic engagement add to those desired traits.

In the end, the public expects the investment in a college education to produce real economic gains above and apart from the benefits of the educational and social attributes resulting from the college experience. The data suggest that the college degree carries a very real economic bonus. For instance, in 2017 dollars, the median annual earnings of full-time workers between the ages of 25 and 37 years were quite skewed by whether or not one had a degree.[8] Those completing the bachelor's degree earned on average $56,000 annually, and those with only a high school degree earned $31,000. Recently, the Social Security Administration demonstrated that the lifetime economic benefit of a college degree is a $900,000 earnings advantage compared with a high school degree. The surplus for those with graduate degrees versus those holding high school degrees is $1.5 million in lifetime median income.[9]

Even with the economic bonus of a college degree, the public trust in higher education is sliding. Once revered for their public role and high integrity, colleges and universities find themselves as suspect. Their long-honored role in American society needs to be restored. Simply relying on their old reputation as engines of economic, scientific, and technological progress and ladders for personal economic mobility is proving inadequate in the public view. In an age of growing distrust of authority and institutions, something much more fundamental must be added to the economic argument if we are to witness higher education ascend in the public eye. It must establish a college education as more than merely a private good for lifetime financial gain. Higher education needs to demonstrate its larger contribution to the cultural, scientific, political, and aesthetic prosperity of the nation. It must become, itself, an agent for civic prosperity and national advancement.

To this end, the realignment with neighborhoods of need that lie within their midst offers colleges and universities the opportunity to regain the civic part of their founding missions. They must become national actors in the long-running American journey to realize racial equity, social justice, and the dream of a long-deferred democracy for all. Knitting together the struggles of universities and these shadow neighborhoods is the pathway to advancement for both. It is, in fact, an American imperative.

In a later chapter, I will attempt to demonstrate how effective, democratically organized university-neighborhood partnerships can open up dramatic pathways for those forgotten children abandoned to poverty and all of its damning pathologies while helping universities foster greater learning and restore their own financial stability.

Notes

1. "A Look at Trends in College Consolidation Since 2016," May 13, 2020, www.educationdive.com.

2. National Association of College and University Business Officers, Tuition Discounting Survey, 2018, www.nacubo.org. See also Nathan D. Grave, *Demographics and the Demand for Higher Education* (Baltimore: Johns Hopkins University Press, 2018).

3. Kim Parker, "The Growing Partisan Divide in Views of Higher Education," Pew Research Center, August 19, 2019, www.pewsocialtrends.org.

4. National Association of College and University Business Officers, Tuition Discounting Survey, 2018.

5. Michael Mitchell, Michael Leuchman, and Kathleen Masterson, *A Lost Decade in Higher Education Funding* (Washington DC: Center on Budget and Policy Priorities, 2017), www.cbpp.org.

6. "Average Student Loan Debt by Year (Graduating Class)," *The College Investor*, December 30, 2019, www.thecollegeinvestor.com.

7. Parker, "The Growing Partisan Divide in Views of Higher Education."

8. Social Security Administration, "Education and Lifetime Earnings," Research, Statistics, and Policy Analysis, November 2015, www.ssa.gov/policy/docs/research-summaries/education-earnings.html.

9. Social Security Administration, "Education and Lifetime Earnings."

3

THE DEMOCRATIC MISSION
OF HIGHER EDUCATION

A merican universities and colleges have always maintained a responsibility for including the preparation of democratic citizens as part of their core mission. As we will see, this commitment has been part of higher education since the American republic was formed, although American universities have at times honored it in name only. Before I turn to that historical record, let's discuss these somewhat odd institutions we call universities.

Today, American colleges and universities are dedicated to the discovery, creation, and dissemination of knowledge. They accomplish these ideals through teaching, scholarship, and service. They offer individuals the opportunity to learn, prepare for careers, and enhance their personal well-being while they widen their understanding of the human experience. They provide learners an opportunity to explore the social institutions that shape our everyday lives while offering a deeper understanding of the natural world they inherit. They introduce students to the ways in which the arts and literature attempt to illuminate the rich variety of cultures that span human existence. Through these broad learning experiences, universities and colleges publicly assert that they are committed to preparing students for their private and public lives. No small part of that institutional claim is universities' contention that their graduates are not just knowledgeable but also capable of a responsible public life within a democratic society. These are values and goals that are omnipresent in American college and university mission statements.

This wasn't always so. Universities came into existence somewhat organically in Western Europe over the course of the twelfth and thirteenth centuries. They began in Paris and Bologna, followed by Naples and Padua. Programs of formal study emerged for interested students, particularly in the areas of law and medicine. Some were outgrowths of cathedrals such as Notre Dame in Paris. Others emerged from royal edicts, as with the founding of the University of Naples by the emperor of the Holy Roman Empire, Frederick II, in 1224.[1] Some had distinctly different origins, in which a gifted teacher typically attracted students to his town to begin their studies. This was the case in Bologna where the teacher Irnerius gathered those interested in the study of law. In all of these origins and for centuries that followed, universities became male sanctuaries prizing learning apart from society and as its own reward. Universities segregated themselves from society. While they featured the study of law and medicine—what we would characterize today as professional education—there was no real sense of these learning communities as examples of a utilitarian education. They were apart from society in conception and public identity.

With the advent of the Enlightenment Age, formal educational study expanded. Reason and science took on elevated status against theology and traditional religious studies. Concepts of freedom and the rise of humanism gave birth to new ideas about social organization and political engagement. As students of Hume, Locke, Rousseau, and Montesquieu, the founders of the American Revolution imagined a republic framed around the values of liberty and equality. They emphasized the importance of popular government, equality before the law for all citizens, and the guarantee of personal liberties.

Their hopes for American democracy would rest with the opinions, beliefs, and participation of its citizens. They firmly espoused the right of the people to shape their government and their society. Their faith in popular sovereignty derived from their deep philosophical beliefs in science and reason guided by moral commitments forged by religious faith. Woven together through the critical institutions of churches and schools, they assumed that these beliefs would increase the probability that popular government would lead to the moral basis of a just and open society.

As romantic ideals of the American Revolution, the republic was founded on slavery and acute class and gender inequality. Nations rarely escape their own contradictions. They become blind to them. Even given these unacceptable contradictions, the founders, however, laid down a vision for a revolutionary and democratic framework for exposing and modifying these obvious inconsistencies surrounding political subordination by race, gender, and class. To realize these democratic ideals, an enlightened citizenry would necessarily depend on the formal education of the American public. In short, democracy and education were now linked inextricably. Preparing an educated citizenry became an essential piece of schooling in the new America. The link between democracy and education was solidly planted as part of the American public narrative. However, it took close to a century for free universal public education to become a reality in the United States.

Ben Franklin was one of the founders of what later became the University of Pennsylvania. He envisioned an institution where intellectual and practical skills would combine, offering a formal education not for some new economic elite but rather "as encouraging and enriching all aspiring young men."[2] Moreover, he hoped for an America where individuals could rise beyond the accidental particulars inherited at their birth. In accordance with his vision, Franklin did not limit his commitment to White men. He started several schools for African Americans.[3] Other founders understood the critical link between an educated citizenry and a stable and successful government based on popular sovereignty. Even Thomas Jefferson and John Adams, the deepest of political rivals, publicly agreed with each other on the necessity of widespread education as essential for democratic governments and the imperative to support it financially.[4] With all of Jefferson's now well-documented failings and contradictions regarding slavery and racial hierarchy, he did profess in *Notes on the State of Virginia* that through education, the people "are the ultimate guardians of their own liberty . . . and we best render them safe."[5]

Clearly, from the origins of the American republic, institutions of higher education accepted as central to their missions the preparation of their students as educated citizens, ready for their roles in their civic and public lives. Colleges and universities have, and continue to maintain, an important role in the development of a democratic civic culture where knowledge and reflection would liberate citizens from merely falling prisoner to their own experience. To be successful, democratic governance requires the eclipse of personal bias born from parochialism. Democracies must be free from those ideologies and movements that only accentuate nativism, social division, and bigotry, all of which are certain pathways to unstable governance.

As we know, Alexander Hamilton and James Madison were deeply wary of a fractured society overwhelmed by majoritarian tyranny. In *The Federalist Papers*, No. 10 and No. 51, they made the case for a federated system of governance, rich with veto points as well as different portals for resolving grievances.[6] They mostly feared a rising tide of majoritarian bias that would eclipse the interests of those in the minority. But they knew that governmental structure by itself would not tame nativist bias. They understood that citizens must be created. Democracy required enlightened leadership and educated publics. By learning what I will call "the arts of democracy" later in this book, engaged students would acquire the essential values and vital skills in forging an inclusive and formidable polity fortified by knowledge, critical reasoning, and wisdom.

Each type of American higher education institution has included in its founding documents some mention of its obligations and contributions to democracy in America. Be it research, moral and ethical teachings, scientific discovery, applied learning, or professional preparation, every type of institution situated itself within the American democratic narrative. From the early universities and colleges, such as Harvard University, Yale University, and The College of William and Mary, to the numerous liberal arts colleges (usually founded by churches), to the land grant state institutions founded by the Morrill Act in 1862, to urban colleges and night schools that were aimed at serving cities flooded with new immigrants, to the advent of community colleges, the institutions specified their contributions to the larger society and in some way to American democracy. All are pledged to use knowledge in service of the public good. The one exception is the current emergence of "for-profit" colleges that are pledged to honor the material interests of their shareholders before anyone else.

Somewhere along the way, universities distanced themselves from their civic mission. It became secondary, if not opaque. While the introduction into the undergraduate curriculum of what we now refer to as liberal or general education appeared following World War II and its frightful expanse of military weaponry and mass human annihilation, the Great Depression largely eclipsed the impulse to broaden American undergraduates and prepare them for an international and democratic perspective. Even the vast patriotic commitment of the national military and civilian sacrifices of World War II did not sustain any renewal of the civic mission of American colleges. In the postwar era, the civic mission yielded to a more secular understanding of the central role of universities and colleges.

The Cold War ushered in two changes. First, there was a heightened regard for the research university model and its contributions to scientific and technological knowledge. At the same time, the modern university was expected to prepare a highly educated workforce in service to a vastly growing corporate sector of the postwar American economy. This is best evidenced by Clark Kerr's famous declaration of the "multiversity." As chancellor of the University of California, Kerr laid out a vision of higher learning as an apparatus attached to the American economy. Be it research, training, or degree completion, among other functions, somehow universities stepped back from their commitment to educating citizens and seemingly showed more interest in providing material services and products for the American economy.

The multiversity was designed as a vast organization acting as a holding company for numerous and disparate schools, institutes, and divisions. It lost much of the historic mission that emphasized the critical role of education for citizenship. Democracy was now at best an afterthought and more likely a shibboleth.[7] This new understanding prioritized the research university as a secular sanctuary. Comprehensive and liberal arts institutions began to emulate this material culture in their pursuit of prestige and reputation, ironically reminiscent of the earliest understanding of places of higher learning as sanctuaries. They all were finding objective purity by distancing themselves from the venality of civic and political life.

Oddly though, in the midst of the immediate aftermath of World War II, President Harry Truman was troubled by a nation having fought through the ravages of the Great Depression only to be followed by the huge impact of the most severe global terror and personal losses experienced from the war. While triumphant and clearly the world's superpower, the United States had glaring inequalities of class and race that were problematic for a nation attempting to redirect its economy, achieve close to a fully employed workforce, and absorb millions of soldiers and previously employed wartime women while avoiding a postwar inflationary spiral. America remained a nation haunted by its indifference to its own contradictions. With these concerns, Truman formed the President's Commission on Higher Education to address the need for the expansion of higher education and the prospect of greater opportunity and access.[8]

The Commission produced a six-volume report, *Higher Education for American Democracy*, published in 1947. While it called for the expansion of higher education and the establishment of a free community college system, the commission called for a true commitment from higher education to move beyond its then-current state as a privileged benefit reserved for those able to afford it to an educational system for all who sought its benefits. Thus, the commission was honoring Franklin's ideal of a university for all who aspire to it. To quote the report,

> The first and most essential charge upon higher education is that at all levels and in all fields of specialization, it shall be the carrier of democratic values, ideals, and process. . . . Only an informed, thoughtful, tolerant people can maintain and develop a free society.[9]

In reality, the bigotry of the nation did not dissipate. From the end of the war through to the current moment, the racial and class inequality persisted, although with courageous moments and movements fighting for deep social change. From the Montgomery bus boycott in Alabama in 1955 and the emergence of Martin Luther King Jr.'s Southern Christian Leadership Conference, to the Freedom Riders and lunch counter sit-ins, to numerous marches, critical civil rights legislation became law in 1965. Despite all of this, racial and class inequality reigned over the nation, and higher education did little to open its doors or change its teaching. The ideals of the founders and the practices of the American republic were in stark contradiction. In spite of the Truman Commission's best intent, the civic mission of higher education was largely opaque at best, while the Jim Crow system of American apartheid persisted in the Southern United States and de facto segregation ruled everywhere else.

Awakenings of the Civic Mission

The 1970s and most of the following decade were witness to the after-math of the campus disruptions of the 1960s and early years of the 1970s. Fearful of being "politicized" again in the post-Vietnam era, institutions of higher education largely sidestepped any proactive role involving civic engagement. Most were taken up with the new phenomenon of endow-ment growth and, later in the 1980s, with the prestige competitions that the imperial impact of the college rankings system fueled. But the 1980s brought important stirrings around the resurrection of the civic responsi-bilities of higher education.

Frustrated by an era celebrating unbridled selfishness under the banner of the Reagan era adoration of the "free market" as the premier arbiter of social value, several university presidents were alarmed by the growing narcissism of their undergraduates. Whatever fears they shared could only have been accel-erated by the popularity of the movie character Gordon Gekko in the film *Wall Street*. Gekko insisted not only that "greed is good" but also that it is the necessary catalyst for growing capitalism and personal satisfaction. In 1985, the presidents of Brown University, Georgetown University, and Stanford University were joined by the former president of the Education Commission of the United States in forming what became Campus Compact. This was envisioned as a national educational declaration to be signed and joined by other university presidents with the express aim of combating the so-called "me generation" and increasing the civic awareness of undergraduates.[10]

The presidents' hopes were modest. They called for the promotion of greater participation in public service and in U.S. elections. They believed the Compact could serve to illustrate and publicize the positive community service of college students. A growing list of presidents joined the Compact in its early years, and the participating colleges and universities champi-oned community service. By 1991, that list grew to 500 participants, and today it stands at nearly 1,000. I had the honor of serving as the chair of the Compact's board of directors during its revitalization in the last decade.

As Compact grew in national presence, the actual organizational work with campuses was formed through state Compacts. The first two began in 1988. They emphasized both student involvement in governmental elections and student volunteerism in poor communities. While the advocacy of community service was and remains a noble practice by itself, it fell far short of the mark required for the dramatic social transformation necessary to reverse racial and class inequality. American cities continued to suffer severe public disinvestment, deindustrialization, and declining employment. Furthermore, the community service begged the question of who was serving whom? Colleges were still largely White institutions with heavily White enrollments while their local neighborhoods were populated by Black and Brown residents who were at the epicenter of urban inequality and racial injustice. Community service was largely staffed by well-meaning White students who would now find their way into assisting the nonprofit institutions with their volunteerism in soup kitchens, after-school programs, and antipoverty centers.

These undergraduates were not truly social change allies, and their efforts could easily be dismissed as the work of rather innocent voyeurs in communities completely foreign to their own largely segregated personal experience. They were discovering the racial and class underbelly of American injustice while two other factors were hidden from view. First, the Black and Brown students of similar age in these communities were neither in colleges nor on their campuses. Second, community service, while noble and appreciated on an individual level, provided only a Band-Aid on a system of structural inequality and institutional racism.

As the Compact matured over the next decade, the inadequacy of the community service approach became evident. "Service learning" emerged. This approach included service field experience within courses that would allow students to deepen their understanding of the underlying issues of poverty, racial segregation, and their economic and social consequences. In the best of this work, the rich analytic and critical material of assigned texts could deepen an understanding of how the structure of political, economic, and social institutions shaped the menu of personal choices and community opportunities for the residents of shadow communities.[11] This clearly was an advance. Eventually, service learning was better understood as part of a commitment to these very neighborhoods. In its more robust intellectual and critical form, it became relabeled as "community-based learning." As we will see in later chapters, even this advance became somewhat eclipsed by a larger vision of this work and of the university's relationships and responsibility. This more encompassing vision of community engagement proved to be more impactful.

As the Compact's perspective grew slowly from volunteerism to engagement in community, other national higher education organizations began their commitments to democratic engagement around racial and gender equality. While not a causal relationship, national organizations focused on the growing presence of students of color on many college campuses. The changing campus sociology certainly created ferment. The statistics on the undergraduate enrollment from 1976 through 2008 capture some of the dynamic.[12] During this period, Black undergraduate enrollment increased from 10 percent of the total to 14 percent of total undergraduate enrollment. White enrollment as a percentage of the total declined from 87 percent to 63 percent. Asian and Pacific students increased six times during this era of change, as did Latino enrollment. Campuses were committed to increasing minority student access, but they were not prepared for the necessary changes this would bring to all aspects of these institutions. Access was not to be the end point in opening up colleges and universities to previously omitted populations. The predominant White middle- and upper-class culture of these institutions would not easily recenter its values, protocols, and traditions, and, most importantly, expand the scope of learning and scholarship. Any number of conflicts challenged campus curriculums, student affairs programs, campus leadership, and the need to dramatically diversify the faculty and administration.

The national higher education organizations began to assert leadership in helping member institutions navigate this new world. The most visionary and courageous, the Association of American Colleges and Universities (AAC&U), under the remarkable leadership of Carol Geary Schneider, launched a visionary national program for faculty and administrators: Engaging Cultural Legacies: Shaping Core Curricula in the Humanities, with funding from the National Endowment for the Humanities (NEH).[13] The program received 250 campus applications for 63 places. Campus teams worked on an intensive curriculum of the latest and best scholarship covering a rich variety of literature outside the traditional Western canon and across a wide spectrum of cultures, global and domestic. One goal was to add to the enduring traditional works with these additional perspectives and histories; another goal was to build more accurate and intellectual frameworks. NEH funded intensive summer residential programs that were as intellectually demanding as any postgraduate seminar. I had the privilege of participating in the program. As a well-read political theorist, I marveled at the breadth of new works, which were all built on the highest scholarly criteria and studied in the best of the liberal arts tradition of critical assessment. The result of Engaging Cultural Legacies was the introduction of curricular initiatives on many campuses. Teachers and scholars expanded their knowledge of the new scholarship around race, gender, and class previously not studied fully in the academy.

As the national political culture wars of the late 1980s and 1990s swelled, right-wing commentators opposed affirmative action and "multicultural-ism" on college campuses. Built on distorted racial stereotypes of intellectual inferiority, the diversification of undergraduate curriculums and increasing college access to long-ignored populations of color were cast as diluting stu-dent entrance requirements, diminishing or destroying traditional curricular requirements, and compromising American democracy by favoring inclusion over merit and excellence.[14]

In the midst of these fierce attacks on campus diversity, AAC&U and its excellent staff, led by Schneider, extended the work initiated with Engaging Cultural Legacies by creating American Commitments: Diversity, Democracy, and Liberal Learning, a ten-year program addressing higher edu-cation's unique role in building a diverse democracy. Once again, faculty and administrators were introduced to the necessary scholarship and the rich his-torical and current literature about communities of color. This work framed a more comprehensive narrative of the promise and pitfalls of American democracy. To Schneider and AAC&U, democracy and diversity are inextri-cably tied together, albeit with a long history of enslavement, nativism, and anti-immigration. If America was to realize its noble but unfulfilled ideals and dreams, then it had to face its past honestly and reaffirm its core values of "liberty and justice for all."

Other significant civic initiatives surfaced during this period. In 1989, a number of leaders of urban universities formed the Coalition of Urban and Metropolitan Universities (CUMU). While not limited to a civic engagement agenda, CUMU's member universities focused on their institutional role as "stewards of place." As cities and suburban communities were engulfed with growing racial and class inequalities, their local universities began to envision a more comprehensive local role. No longer content to be sanctuaries within the metropolitan core, CUMU reestablished a larger civic mission for its member institutions. This new civic model grew exponentially in the second decade of the twenty-first century. I had the privilege of serving and chair-ing CUMU's Board of Directors during that period. Its brilliant executive director, Bobbi Laur, grew the membership from a few dozen universities to almost one hundred.

CUMU is now a major force in reestablishing and expanding higher education's role in directly addressing racial and class inequality both on and off campus. The initial founding and the later maturation of CUMU and its commitment to "place" for higher education serve as an important landmark in this work because the community, along with the preparation of undergraduates as civically engaged actors, became equally important.

In 1998, AAC&U created an additional initiative specific to the expansion of learning, teaching, and scholarship of race. Racial Legacies and Learning set up a vast number of dialogues and seminars that deepened the capacity of universities around the understanding and history of race as a unique category of human experience and most assuredly of American history. Suddenly there were a number of civic approaches growing around the higher education sector. In 2003, the Association of State Colleges and Universities (ASCU), in partnership with *The New York Times*, introduced The American Democracy Project (ADP) for its 250 public institutions. ADP concentrated on building the knowledge and democratic practice of state university students and eventually grew into a forty-six-state program of civic education and public dialogues.

Later, in 2011, a group of community colleges formed The Democracy Commitment (CDC), aimed at the fastest and largest enrollment sector in higher education. Community colleges are more diverse in every category than other higher education sectors but largely ignored by them. They are chronically stereotyped as merely job preparation institutions. Rarely are they valued as critical agencies for supporting and preparing students for civic and political roles in their communities, which often are located in the critical arenas of racial and class inequities.

At the turn of the twentieth century, under the leadership of Eugene Lange, philanthropist and longtime board chair of Swarthmore College, a number of private residential liberal arts colleges formed Project Pericles. As president of Wagner College, I was asked to join this coalition of civic-minded institutions that was committed to educating students for political and civic participation. Lange took inspiration from the Ancient Greek classic by Thucydides, *History of the Peloponnesian War*, where the Athenian general Pericles offers a robust defense of democracy during his famed funeral oration. While a small cohort compared with AAC&U's 1,500-plus institutional members and ASCU's large membership, Project Pericles represented an influential grouping. The Council of Independent Colleges, a national association of small private colleges founded in 1956, joined the renewal of the civic mission around this same period.

With the acceptance and acceleration of community-based learning and student involvement in community service, the emergence of campus dialogues around race and inclusion, and the swelling of numerous movements to broaden and defend racial, gender, and LGBTQ rights, the work was contributing to a new, broader, and inclusive vision for American democracy. In some ways this coagulated with the successful presidential campaign of Barack Obama. While some earlier critics were describing the withdrawal of Americans into the immediate and material enclaves of personal life and segregated communities, something was bubbling on American campuses.

This renewal of the civic mission, however, was unfocused, sometimes idiosyncratic, and often isolated within the participating campuses. It remained fragmented, and, most importantly, higher education's civic renewal was limited for at least two major reasons. First, this work was still about educating students to be engaged citizens. It was not focused on community impact, not to mention any wholesale movement calling for a major social attack on racial and class inequality. Too much of the work was about transforming university students and not about any significant commitment to transforming neighborhoods.

In all my work with national higher education organizations in this period, and often still in the present, higher education was deeply uncomfortable moving outside its own political lane. This comes from years of comfort in defining the role of American universities as independent arbiters of objectivity. It is the kind of objectivity that finds solace in effecting a culture of scholarship and teaching as "impartial" while ignoring that this sort of equivalence only reproduces the social status quo, one steeped in racial injustice, gender bias, and class subordination. The objective facts are clear. The United States remains far from its democratic ideals. The objective facts illustrate a political and social universe of racial segregation that has dramatic consequences for neighborhoods, churches, schools, and, most importantly, opportunity. We need the type of intellectual and academic objectivity that does not excuse universities from meeting the promise of inclusive and equitable democracy. They have direct responsibility to use knowledge to serve the founding ideals of this nation.

Second, the civic renewal of higher education missed the mark in this period precisely because it did not see the necessary link between racial justice and democratic progress. Diversity and democracy are inextricably linked in the American narrative, but campuses divide them into separate commitments that have distinct administrative homes and often are divided into separate academic disciplines.

In short, the civic renewal remained a palliative approach. At worst, it did not rise above deploying civic engagement into economically distressed communities. Universities and colleges could be criticized for becoming voyeuristic and utilitarian in teaching students about inequality and racial injustice while not fully allying the institutions with these neighborhoods. They did collaborate with their community partners in directly addressing the persistent injustice of it all. At best, the civic renewal remained a well-intentioned, somewhat politically modest, if not naive, attempt at changing America. Much more was needed.

Major Steps Forward

The first sparks for building a vision of campuses and neighborhoods allying in common cause in the practice of joining democracy and diversity showed up with two major advances. I will address them in nonchronological order. On January 10, 2012, AAC&U's National Task Force on Civic Learning and Democratic Engagement, of which I was a member, presented its report at the White House. This was a seminal moment in the recognition of higher education's direct role in renewing the promise and practice of a more inclusive American democracy.

Under the guidance of AAC&U President Schneider, and with the diligence and elegance of our principal author, Caryn McTighe Musil, we produced a critical report, *A Crucible Moment: College Learning and Democracy's Future.* It marks an inflection point in both chronicling and defining higher education's commitment and practice of civic engagement. Resurrecting President Truman's Commission on Higher Education and its goals for expanding higher education as a necessary element for America's political stability and economic growth in the post-World War II era, *A Crucible Moment* illustrated that the civic mission of higher education was expected at the very founding of the republic.

Quite opposite to the modern notions of the university as a secular and separate enclave within a democratic society, universities were meant to play a critical role in America's experiment in popular government. What *A Crucible Moment* achieved was a careful and precise set of values, protocols, and practices for defining the appropriate role and substance of civic learning in America for the twenty-first century. Apart from settling for the limited understanding of democracy as reduced to a system of governmental and electoral rules that produce laws and legislation for selecting and sustaining popular government, the report did not separate democratic government from democratic society. Government and civil society constitute two equal parts of the democratic equation, and the national task force did not divorce the social realities of racial, gender, and class inequalities from this larger political vision.

In *A Crucible Moment*, the national task force sought to capture the civic stirrings that evoked this larger perspective of politics and society. It captured the enormous amount of civic activity already underway in and around universities and colleges in the United States, although it warned of a "civic recession" in the larger context of the American polity. The report included a generous catalog of numerous national and some regional organizations supporting civic engagement in higher education, but it mainly focused on defining civic learning, its best practices, and how to assess it.

This provided clarity by separating isolated community service and volunteerism from civic learning, which required civic field experience joined to formal study and intentional reflection. Learning is growth in understanding a subject, and civic learning couples text with experience. Learning is derived by the making of meaning from sustained reflection by comparing and contrasting one with the other. For instance, if students are enrolled in a sociology course on American poverty and urban life, they may learn more if they are placed in field experiences that mirror the substantive texts about urban poverty. But if these students are never asked to carefully reflect on their field experiences in light of the assigned texts, they likely will miss out on how each can expand an understanding of why such poverty persists. They could fail to find the limits, if not bias, in some of the texts themselves. Or they may simply reproduce their own stereotypes about poor communities because they never gained a greater perspective from the texts themselves.

Without critically assessing the interplay of texts and field work, one would seriously question what level of civic learning is taking place. However noble the intentions of the instructor, this sort of all-too-familiar encounter with service learning does not educate students for democratic citizenship. In many cases, it leads to a reproduction of class and race stereotypes as often as it reveals them. These types of shallow civic learning were held up to the light in *A Crucible Moment*, and the report offered a sophisticated set of pedagogical practices for accomplishing genuine civic learning.

While the thrust of the report illustrated comprehensive civic learning and civic engagement, the primary emphasis was on intellectually and operationally defining civic learning of university students. The campus was its primary arena. This in and of itself was a critical advance in the field and should not be understood as anything but a major breakthrough in grounding this work in the classrooms and corridors of learning in higher education. But the report did open the door to the community. It expanded the conversation so that neighborhoods became locations of reciprocal learning for civic growth. The expansion of civic leadership and educational opportunity within the community became a part of higher education's measurement of the value and success of its civic engagement initiatives. When *A Crucible Moment* was launched at the Obama White House, I sensed that we had broadened higher education's standard for civic engagement. We were broadening the circle of its institutional stakeholders by prioritizing the impact of civic engagement on the local neighborhoods, not simply measured by the improvement in student civic participation. The door was opening.

In this same period, a second major breakthrough began the alignment of universities with the civic, economic, and political prosperity of their local neighborhoods. This proved to be a formidable reconceptualization of community and campus, namely the formulation of universities as "anchor institutions" in the neighborhoods they inhabit. Anchor colleges and universities moved to become "stewards of place" and not accidental residents divorced from their communities. They are geographical entities, and they function as communities due to the critical roles played by schools, churches, libraries, local businesses, and foundations as well as a host of nonprofit organizations in the arts, public service, and recreation. All served as important entities embedded or anchored in these very neighborhoods. Envisioning colleges and universities as important neighborhood actors, for better or worse, expands the civic theater for higher education.

The anchor model emerges from the genius of several longtime civic and transformational leaders in higher education. First among them is Ira Harkavy from the University of Pennsylvania. Long ensconced in directing several decades of a remarkable partnership between West Philadelphia and the university, Harkavy led a group of like-minded colleagues to respond to a 2008 call for proposals from the U.S. Department of Housing and Urban Development (HUD) to deepen the impact of educational and medical institutions on addressing urban problems. The appointees of the newly elected Obama administration were hungry for innovative approaches to the dilemmas of failing schools and the persistent coefficients of health disparities in poor urban neighborhoods.

Forming an anchor task force, Harkavy and his colleagues proposed the new model in their report, *Anchor Institutions as Partners in Building Successful Communities and Local Economies.*[15] The significance of the introduction of the anchor concept cannot be overstated. Suddenly, university-based, civically engaged work had a framework for connecting campus and community as equal partners. It offered a means to align higher education with other neighborhood anchor partners in a vision of common responsibility for advancing the civic prosperity of the physical space they shared.

The derivation of this anchor work actually lies in the Clinton administration's 1994 creation of the Office of University Partnerships (OUP) as part of HUD. Then the hope was that these partnerships would bring new allies to the table in engaging longstanding urban deficits. The sad truth is that from the very inception of the office, OUP has been underfunded and underutilized. It did, however, establish the important link between campus and community. The advent of the anchor concept was necessary to provide the inspiration for a truly democratic vision of what is now a partnership model where anchors become allies to long-ignored communities, and these neighborhoods become allies in helping universities rediscover their civic roots.

The Movement to Anchor Partnerships

In short order, the concept of anchor partnerships has become universal within the civic engagement movement. Both domestically and internationally, the anchor institution concept has framed both progressive and lesser reform efforts for increasing civic and economic prosperity. I will spend more time on particular examples of the anchor model in later chapters. For now, suffice it to say that the anchor model became the most advanced formulation of the civic mission of universities and colleges in this era of American higher education. It restored the original democratic ideal articulated by Franklin and Jefferson. The anchor model brings us the substance of this book, namely the direct role of colleges and universities in building a democratic culture and in addressing the current social barriers to achieving its promise of social inclusion, equal opportunity, and an engaged, knowledgeable, and ethical polity.

Notes

1. Charles Homer Haskins, *The Rise of Universities* (Ithaca, NY: Cornell University Press, 1923); Ian McNeely, *Reinventing Knowledge: From Alexandria to the Internet* (New York: Norton Press, 2008).

2. Walter Isaacson, *Benjamin Franklin: An American Life* (New York: Simon & Schuster, 2003), 149–150.

3. National Task Force for Civic Learning and Democratic Education, *A Crucible Moment* (Washington DC: Association of American Colleges and Universities, 2012), 17. See also Ira Harkavey and Matthew Hartley, "Pursuing Franklin's Democratic Vision for Higher Education," *Peer Review* 10, no. 23 (Spring/Summer 2008).

4. Andrew Delbanco, *College: What It Was and Should Be* (Princeton, NJ: Princeton University Press, 2012), 28.

5. Cited in Benjamin Barber, *An Aristocracy for Everyone* (New York: Ballantine Books, 1992), 283.

6. Alexander Hamilton, James Madison, and John Jay, *The Federalist: A Collection of Essays* (Mineola, NY: Dover Publications, 2014).

7. Clark Kerr, *The Uses of the University* (Cambridge, MA: Harvard University Press, 2001).

8. National Task Force for Civic Learning and Democratic Education, *A Crucible Moment*, 18.

9. National Task Force for Civic Learning and Democratic Education, *A Crucible Moment*, 18; and The President's Commission on Higher Education, Washington DC, 1947, Vol. 1.

10. "History of Campus Compact," www.compact.org.

11. Richard Guarasci and Grant Cornwell, *Democratic Education in an Age of Difference* (San Francisco: Jossey-Bass, 1997); Richard Guarasci and David Mapstone, "Intercultural Citizenship and Democratic Sensibility at Hobart and William Smith Colleges," in *To Serve and Learn*, ed. Joseph L. DeVitis, Robert W. Johns, and Douglas J. Simpson (New York: Peter Lang Publishers, 1998), 47–62; and Richard Guarasci, "Civic Engagement and Higher Learning," in Joseph L. DeVitis and Pietro Sasso, *Higher Education and Society* (New York: Peter Lang Publishers, 2016), 61–80.

12. National Center for Education Statistics, July 2010, section 24.1, www.nces.ed.gov.

13. Carol Geary Schneider, "Cultural Pluralism and Civic Values," *Liberal Education* 90, no. 3 (Summer 2004).

14. Alan Bloom, *The Closing of the American Mind* (New York: Simon & Schuster, 1987).

15. An instructive analysis of this position can be found in Robert Putnam, *Bowling Alone: The Collapse and Revival of the American Community* (New York: Simon & Schuster, 2000). See also Robert Putnam, *Our Kids: The American Dream in Crisis* (New York: Simon & Schuster, 2015).

4

DEMOCRATIC EDUCATION
AND CIVIC PURPOSE

Civic work starts with student and community learning. Civic learning is essential for engagement and ultimately transformation. It builds the values, knowledge, skills, and practices that develop young leaders on university and college campuses and in the community.

Civic learning also affects many others. It broadens the intellectual and emotional depth of participating faculty members, engaged administrators and staff, community partners, and neighborhood leaders. They learn more about their respective cultural legacies, individual biographies, and the institutional barriers that frame their everyday lives and personal aspirations. When civic practice is organized around democratic principles, it offers the possibility of significant progress. All engaged stakeholders move from being participants to becoming allies. They reach across the wide racial and class disparities that frame contemporary American life. Strangers become partners in their common pursuit of neighborhoods and campuses that are moving together toward racial equity and social justice.

In my experience, the most comprehensive form of civic learning occurs in the sustained work within campus and community partnerships. It can occur in other field placements when attended to with care, respectful field work, and serious personal reflection. In any of these settings, participants are more likely to develop what I term the arts of democracy: development of active listening and active voice, establishment of empathy and reciprocity, acquisition of intercultural competency, use of mediation and negotiation skills, understanding of ambiguity and nuance, and learning the necessity of building coalitions as pathways to solutions and action. Through sustained civic practice, tempered with an openness to learning, I have witnessed students and community residents develop these critical skills.

As an educator, I know this type of experience opens up deep learning. A former student of mine when I was a dean at Hobart and William Smith Colleges during the 1990s illustrates this learning. Kendra, a White senior undergraduate, was intelligent, self-confident, and well read. She defined herself as a feminist in the sense that she was in charge of her own life. She came from an economically comfortable background. She enrolled in my "Politics, Community, and Service" class fully prepared to encounter and critically interrogate the readings around democracy, diversity, and inclusion. To many she appeared to be a wonderful recipient of a fine undergraduate education. She was open to different points of view while maintaining a strong commitment to justice and equity. She was the type of student her teachers would view with pride when she eventually walked across the stage at commencement. They would be confident that she would soon make her mark in the world.

For her civic field work in my course, Kendra was placed at a residential drug recovery center for mothers and their children. The minimum residency was three months. Most of the residents came from New York City, Albany, Syracuse, Rochester, Buffalo, and other urban settings in New York State. Almost all of them were women of color. To Kendra's great surprise, they were mostly younger than her twenty-one years.

In my class, students did the usual reading, wrote essays, and took exams, but they also kept a three-part dialogical journal and they completed the semester with a citizenship autobiography. The journal asked them to enter reactions to the readings (e.g., what do you want to ask or say to the author?), then chronicle that week's field experience and compare and contrast the first two parts. We would share some of these reflections in class. The citizenship autobiography asked students to work through the prism of the texts and field experience, and answer the question, "Who were they becoming as democratically engaged students?"

Kendra began to work closely with one young mother in particular. They were so different in so many ways. One was a young mom trapped in unforgiving economic circumstances typical of racially segregated inner-city neighborhoods while the other was successfully completing a four-year degree at a highly selective college. One was a mother with limited choices and the other had seemingly open vistas in front of her. Both had good hearts but likely radically different futures born from radically different circumstances. At the conclusion of the course, this is what Kendra wrote in her citizenship autobiography in response to the question, "Who are you becoming?"

We are a year apart and somehow she seemed so much older than me. She was burdened with responsibilities I could never dream of having. She was born into very unfortunate circumstances that made her life much more difficult and frustrating than most could ever tolerate. I felt so spoiled, so unaware that lives like hers are endured daily. I felt sorry for the childhood she never had and deserved. I thought of the accident that occurred almost 22 years ago when she was born into her life and I into mine. It seemed so unfair and cruel. I thought a lot about God that night.[1]

Kendra demonstrated how deep civic engagement nurtures the qualities of empathy and reciprocity through active listening. In addition, the intercultural experience helped Kendra significantly expand her understanding of economic inequality, institutional racism, and gender subordination well beyond what normally is available in a traditional seat-time course. Even though the assigned readings engaged these topics in detail, Kendra's personal encounter heightened the depth of understanding. These social inequalities were exposed in very real terms. And for our young mom, the veil was pulled back on the possibilities of greater opportunities that should be available to her as well. These women developed a human bond that deepened their respective understanding of systems of injustice that framed their personal choices.

But on further inspection, my community-based learning course was itself burdened by its own limitations. Like most of these types of courses, it is a stand-alone experience. As powerful as these experiences may be, the civic work begins and ends with the given semester. While Kendra and the other students in that class demonstrated remarkable learning, they would move on. The community remained. For our young mother, maybe another Kendra would come along, but most likely not. In other words, as elegant a learning experience as these courses can be when managed responsibly and comprehensively by the professor, students, and community partners, they privilege the civic growth of the college student. They are not without advancing empathy, voice, and some of the other arts of democracy among the community participants, but the entire project is devoid of the larger strategic need to change the circumstances that produce such skewed class, gender, and race outcomes in the first place. Community-based learning courses are necessary but not sufficient. That project demands the expanded alignment of universities and neighborhoods in order to enhance the possibilities for the social transformation of both the campus and the community.

In contrast, student experiences with the Wagner College-Port Richmond Partnership (PRP) were sustained, year-round commitments. The PRP provided community-engaged courses for both college and high school students. The courses, however, were only a part of the much larger partnership that included a five-sector approach in college readiness programs (K–16), immigration justice, community arts and humanities, economic and local business development, and health service aimed at reducing health disparities. The participating community partners included more than twenty institutions ranging from public and charter schools, hospitals, and nonprofit health providers to arts institutions, government offices, local bank foundations, and a range of other nonprofit antipoverty organizations. College and high school students, and to a lesser degree their middle school and elementary counterparts, are engaged in ongoing projects that are not bound by semesters. They are linking formal learning with civic engagement where the arts of democracy form the real curriculum. They are learning to become leaders for a just, equitable, and inclusive public order, and they are part of the attempted renaissance of the Port Richmond neighborhood and its nearby college partner, Wagner.

In chapter 1, I introduced you to Mindy, one of the PRPLA graduates and now a graduate of Wagner College. Mindy and the eleven other PRPLA members have had a more comprehensive experience than the random community-based learning course could offer. They have been part of the partnership since they were fifteen years old. The community-based learning courses are important introductions to the arts of democracy, but they are just that—introductions. I will offer a full description of the Port Richmond/ Wagner College Partnership in chapter 6.

Civic learning should be a subset of a larger educational frame, namely democratic education. This more comprehensive approach assumes, as educational reformer John Dewey did, that democracy itself is much greater than the mere design of government and its assemblages of executive, legislative, and judicial agencies. To Dewey, democracy was first and foremost "a mode of associated living."[2] He meant that democracy is a lived, dynamic set of relationships and experiences framed around the core beliefs of popular sovereignty, personal liberty, and equality before the law. The architecture of government is a means to render these values.

For the engines of government to work democratically, they require a democratic culture. How we live together democratically as a sovereign society requires the freedom to think critically, reserving not only the right of inquiry but also the means to investigate and evaluate laws, policies, and political behavior. For these civic traits to flourish, education needs to be organized around specific pedagogical methods and clear learning outcomes. Among them I would list critical thinking as opposed to rote learning.

Democratic education is about developing engaged citizens as full participants in the public life of society. This type of education values learners as active agents in gaining knowledge through the interplay of ideas, direct experience, and deep reflection. In addition, preparing students as engaged citizens for a democratic culture requires the development of effective communication skills, both oral and written. These skills support the active voice necessary for full democratic participation.

Such citizens must be able to understand and negotiate social difference and cultural diversity. They need a competency in understanding the natural world and its physical environments. Students must learn how the structure of institutional authority frames the agenda of personal opportunities, racial destinies, and class configurations. They must have a fluency in the making of social, cultural, and personal meanings. The arts, humanities, and technologies are the grammar and vocabularies in which we interpret the human experience and its surrounding social forces.

To foster democracy, civic learning has some concrete predicates that should be manifested in the forms of learning and in the system of education. Those previously listed are all requisite. They are commonly associated with liberal education, the form of learning that is not "liberal" or "conservative" in the popular American political vernacular but rather liberal in the sense that it "liberates" the learners from being merely prisoners of their own parochialism. It develops methods for the learners to be engaged in uncovering the larger worlds that surround them. They become more worldly or cosmopolitan, that is to say more comfortable with encountering the unfamiliar, the unknown, the stranger. They learn about complexity and nuance in treating any particular problem or experience.

These are the democratic traits that one can gain from civic experience, especially when it is founded on the skills of inquiry and reflection embedded in liberal education. I find these attributes are more likely to be located within civic learning, in particular, and when they are part of anchor partnerships. They are quite powerful in advancing democratic learning and democratic citizenship, and most importantly, when they become learning outcomes for all K–16 students and community leaders and residents as well. Democracy, learning, and engaged citizenship are best forged together when they are part of movements for social transformation.

Becoming Transformational Leaders

For this nation to overcome its inherent institutionalized racism and deep class divisions embedded throughout American society, our educational system must develop a generation of transformational leaders. Toward this end, these leaders must be educated about the values and practices necessary to support a democracy. They must be knowledgeable about the history, failures, and progress of this nation. To achieve this goal, they need to be experienced in the methods of democratic learning. These leaders must ascend from these shadow neighborhoods, armed with the arts of democracy and the wisdom gained from the practices experienced in these early years with democratic partnerships.

My efforts in designing and sustaining the PRP were my best work in democratic education. Having been an active teacher in community-based learning from the early 1990s and well into my Wagner years as provost and then president, I came to see its limits. I wondered how higher education, and Wagner College in particular, could take on a more strategic role in their local communities. The neighborhood partnership concept seemed to be the most comprehensive approach. Toward this end, my staff and I put together meetings with Port Richmond leaders from local schools, public offices, religious and economic organizations, and the nonprofit sector. Soon thereafter, Wagner College decided to partner with this particular neighborhood community.

The neighborhood is distinctive. Staten Island was settled in 1666. For most of its history before and after the incorporation of the five boroughs into New York City in 1898, Staten Island was labeled a semi-rustic getaway from Manhattan and Brooklyn. The opening of the Verrazano-Narrows Bridge in 1964 allowed New Yorkers looking for a suburban opportunity to find more open spaces and private homes inside the confines of New York City proper. Its population currently stands at just under 500,000. On the island, Port Richmond is a neighborhood approximately two miles from the Wagner campus. For much of its distinct history, it was the home of European immigrants, but now Mexicans account for well over 50 percent of its 11,000 residents. Some are now citizens. The remainder of the neighborhood is made up of African Americans and working-class White New Yorkers.

Port Richmond hurts from all the wounds found in low-income Brown and Black communities. Health disparities and K–12 school metrics are at the low end of the scale. While rich with cultural vitality, there are limited outlets for expressing the compelling narratives of its residents. And in an age of punishing realities for undocumented immigrants and for African American youth, the opportunities for change appear to be remote. Despite Port Richmond's public image to some on Staten Island, the vast majority of its residents are multigenerational families best characterized by their strong work ethic, family loyalty, and unbreakable resiliency. I believed deeply in the richness of their respective cultural legacies. I saw firsthand that Port Richmond has greatly untapped economic, civic, and cultural capacity.

One morning, I visited a local charter school, New World Prep, that Wagner helped to found in Port Richmond. New World Prep was started as a public charter middle school to assist immigrant children. Its core mission is framed around equity and excellence, and it is now a resounding success story. When the school started, it flew on a wing and a prayer. As I toured the facilities, it was obvious this school would have to fight for its existence because of a tough neighborhood; many novice, at best, English speakers; and new, very young teaching staff.

I was taken to one middle-school classroom where the teacher was a recent Wagner graduate and former member of the football team. What happened next stunned me. The fact that the middle-school students were presenting their "hypotheses" for their research papers was enough to surprise me, but then I watched presenters, one more impressive than the next, stand up with confidence and passion to defend their theses. In the middle of this poor diverse community in a dilapidated building located in a shadow neighborhood, my spirits were soaring with delight. In full view was the inescapable evidence of the untapped creativity and unquenched thirst for knowledge from children long ignored on this island and in this city. So little is expected of them and, consequently, will they come to expect so little of themselves? They were poster children for those who would redline their hopes and dreams by creating and ignoring obstacles that deprived so many of them of future success.

I knew what lay ahead of them on the streets. They would soon face a litany of challenges from chronic poverty, parental and personal unemployment, violence, racial stereotyping, gender subordination, anti-immigrant policies from federal authorities, and so many other barriers to success and upward mobility. Turning to my guide, I said, "These children are so excited, but I can see that life is about to become very difficult for them." I thought about how many will make it through high school, how many will survive the streets, and how many will be caught in the web of intergenerational poverty. And this is how it goes in the Port Richmonds of the world. Right then, I said, "How can we let this country discard so many of these children?" I knew immediately this was not just a cause for a good college, founded on a sound moral vision. This was an imperative for all colleges to become allies in building a truly pluralistic democracy in America. We should do this in order to redeem all of our founding missions.

We built the PRP and within it we founded the PRPLA to support college readiness for those performing below that level as they entered PRHS. Eventually we added the middle school and elementary feeder schools into our work. I will describe all of this in chapter 6 when I chronicle examples of comprehensive partnerships. While college readiness is the proximate goal of this highly successful program, the larger political one is the development of an interracial generation of transformative leaders in their chosen professions and in their communities.

We organized teaching and learning with a democratic pedagogy for the PRPLA students and their Wagner College student mentors. In part, this was in tandem with the four-year undergraduate curriculum required for all Wagner students pursuing a bachelor's degree. The Wagner Plan for the Practical Liberal Arts was launched in 1997 under my leadership as provost. It is built on a curricular architecture that combines cohort and experiential learning.[3] It is based on the principle of learning by doing where "reading, writing, and doing" are included within three distinct semesters out of the eight required for the degree. For many Wagner students, the experiential learning component is a civic initiative linked to the course subjects and texts, similar to community-based learning.

PRPLA was based on the same pedagogy but with the explicit focus on building leadership capacity among the high school and college students in the program. My goal was to see them introduced to the arts of democracy through the combination of linking their classroom work in their on-campus summers with the civic initiatives in Port Richmond. We taught them to locate and plot the assets contained within their community and to imagine them as stepping-stones for building social change. These high school students were not simply listening to a lecture but were asked to engage the course materials critically and use them in reflection about the purpose and value of the field work. We expected them to become leaders for positive change. Later in the PRP history, we expanded the program to include elementary and middle school students in their own PRP educational tracks. They, too, were taught democratically about academic excellence, positive community leadership, and the social value of civic engagement. We were teaching all of these students, from elementary through college, about the theory and practice of American democracy while engaging their communities in democratic practice.

Work and Democracy: Becoming Civic Professionals

Democratic education is not merely a four-year internship during the undergraduate years. It is a disposition toward living and learning throughout one's life. We can envision how our campus and community partners will function in their political lives as actively engaged citizens, but what of their work lives where so much of their existence will be spent? Is there no relationship between work and democracy? How do we reconcile these two realms? What is the larger social vision for democratic practice? Does democracy stop at the door of one's workplace or profession? Is the workplace exempt from democratic experience?

As a longtime dedicated faculty member and progressive administrator, I had the privilege of educating thousands of students. I became attached to them as intellects as well as people. I cared deeply about preparing them with a formidable education. All had dreams and aspirations for creating meaningful careers for themselves. I did, too. The question was, how would they find a way to link their democratic sensibilities into this part of their lives? It wasn't as if all were to become formally drawn into political careers. How could they relate their chosen undergraduate concentrations or other related passions with a democratic work life?

I was not unfamiliar with the history and sociology of work as academic disciplines. During my years as a political science professor, I collaborated with thoughtful and generous colleagues in designing and teaching in a program called Work and Society. The courses ranged across the disciplines in history, sociology, economics, political science, literature, film, and art. I found my unique contribution by introducing courses on democracy and work. In part, my students and I would study the many experiments in workplace democracy in Sweden, Israel, England, Japan, and the United States.[4] This was a fabulous course, organized with significant elements of democratic practice for students as they became responsible, in part, for assessing each other's work. The students found acting responsibly and democratically was just as hard as it was depicted in the literature citing industrial workplaces.

All of this is to say that I was not unfamiliar with connecting democracy and work, particularly in the American experience. So it was with great enjoyment that I stumbled across a wonderful book by Bill Sullivan titled *Work and Integrity*.[5] Writing about the dysfunction that occurred in U.S. professions, Sullivan chronicles how licensed professionals, such as medical, nursing, and law, were given certain privileges if they developed strict codes of conduct and care. Embedded in these professional codes were the expectation and accountability for ethical standards. These rules connected the professions to their respective publics such as patients, clients, and students.

What Sullivan elegantly traces is the separation of the professions and their publics as the former became protective of their own self-interests. This resulted in a transactional relationship instead of the former vision of professionals' primary responsibility for the intimate care of their publics. Sullivan went on to explain how the professions became interest groups advocating for their need for regulatory protection from their publics. They sought limited liability in the practice of their work. They organized into associations and later many joined traditional trade unions, primarily entangled in wages and hours conflicts.

With this work, Sullivan was hoping to underscore professionals' loss of integrity as they became more and more concerned with self-interest and more distanced from their patients, clients, students, and so forth. He advocated for the reconciliation between professionals and publics in what he came to conceptualize as "civic professionalism."

When I read this book in the mid-1990s, I was struck by two issues. First, Sullivan did not include a study of the university's professorate and its civic professionalism. For too long, academics were magnetically drawn to their identification with their disciplines and less to their students. Shouldn't higher education interrogate its own practices and review its primary allegiances? Was it to scholarship or teaching? Research or students? I had answers to those questions, but I also held a much larger vision of how to tie work and democracy together in a meaningful way for my students. It also opened me up to thinking about a much larger understanding of how to unite the long-standing university fault lines between the liberal arts and the sciences on one hand and the professional and applied fields on the other. Since the publication of *The Two Cultures and the Scientific Revolution*, the famous work by C.P. Snow, these two realms of academic study have remained estranged.[6]

I became enchanted with Sullivan's concept of civic professionalism. It provided an elegant conceptualization that allowed all types of work to be understood as service to their respective publics. This approach allowed me to teach students that every type of career has a corresponding public that depends on their service or product. From this perspective, my students were extending their democratic practice with communities of need into public lives of engaged democratic work.

If my students went on to the helping professions, their civic professionalism was self-evident. As nurses, doctors, teachers, and so on and as people of democratic conscience, their civic professionalism is self-evident. But what about the more secular disciplines? Those entering the world of science can make a clear case for their democratic sensibility depending on how and where they practice scientific work. Medical, environmental, and climate sciences are examples of potentially civic-purposed work. Even a college major like finance retains a civic purpose if students can imagine that the mobilization of capital for public purpose can assist community challenges.

The essential point is that the concept of civic professionalism provided my students with a bridge to link their future careers with the larger democratic project. This linking of work and democracy becomes a critical element of connecting work, education, and civic purpose.

For me, the concept goes further. Becoming a civic professional means practicing one's craft with a deep respect for the publics served. This ultimately requires a high level of intentionality in the actual work. It means interpreting the social context of the production, location, and distribution of the product. It requires critical thinking about the enterprise and the profession. Social and cultural elements are in play. All of this requires reflection. This type of introspection calls up another key concept in democratic work: reflective practice.

In 1983, Don Schon published his classic work in this field, *The Reflective Practitioner: How Professionals Think in Action.*[7] He wanted to end the artificial separation between the arts and sciences as intellectual learning as opposed to applied learning as utilitarian and devoid of intellectual character. He illustrated his argument by demonstrating the interpretative, critical, and reflective efforts in architecture, engineering, health care, and counseling. Each juxtaposes well-verified theory with the inelegant particulars of the real variables in play in that field. The variables never fit exactly, and these professions always must apply the skills of liberal learning if one is to get the bridge built, the patient diagnosed correctly, and the surgical procedure diagrammed to fit the actual physiology of the patient.

Schon's pioneering work opens up the second challenge in linking work and democracy and the concept of civic professionalism. His ability to convincingly demonstrate the intellectual (i.e., interpretive) content in applied work assisted me in understanding how to reconcile the two estranged realms of academic work, namely the liberal arts and the applied fields. For me, a symbiotic relationship exists between them. In democratic education, one needs to combine learning and doing, analysis and action, critical thinking, and the arts of democracy.

It became obvious to me and my faculty colleagues that the professional programs needed the basic elements of the arts and sciences in order to educate their graduates as reflective practitioners. Teachers, nurses, physician assistants, and premed students all needed a substantive acquaintance with the rich cultural histories that will present themselves to these students. They required the skills of liberal education to correctly analyze the best practices in successfully applying their knowledge in service to others. In highly diverse workplaces where collaboration and personal trust will be essential, our business students needed all of these traits to be successful. In short, the need for the liberal arts and sciences was clear for the professional programs.

The challenge was to demonstrate that liberal arts and science students need the applied areas while also ensuring that liberal arts and science faculties and their students see this culture of applied learning as impera-tive. Toward this end, we asked why a humanities student wouldn't need to understand the dynamic elements and relationships in business, health care, and so on. Since so much of the humanities and the performing arts are set in these very contexts, how could these learners be denied a true understanding of the tensions, conflicts, and choices embedded in these worlds if they were to make meaning of them? So much of reality lives in the applied professions. The liberal arts and professional programs are less remote than once imagined. To succeed in many careers, young profession-als need the skills to work across disciplines while employing the intellec-tual breadth gained from the liberal arts and the practical imagination from the applied disciplines.

From this perspective, the reconciliation of the two cultures became the foundation for what I titled the Wagner Plan for the Practical Liberal Arts. Democratic education begins with the learner's active voice, which is more fully discovered within the social context of intellectual and practical engage-ment. From this orientation, it became essential for me to build an under-graduate curriculum around problem-centered learning communities linked to civically engaged experiential learning. This became the general education program required for the undergraduate degree at Wagner College beginning in 1998 and continuing today. Enveloped within a rich commitment to the diversity of cultural legacies and the social experiences of self-discovery, this curriculum was a first step in providing students with many of the elements of educational preparation for developing engaged citizens.

What followed the introduction of the Wagner Plan, of course, was the design and implementation of the PRP. Together, we began to assemble the vital elements needed to prepare a new generation for a truly inclusive democracy. We added the dynamic Bonner Leaders Program, which trained undergraduates as intercultural civic leaders and active agents for substantive social change. I will describe the Bonner model in chapter 8.

We developed the partnership in the five sectors mentioned earlier in this chapter. We dug deeper into the college readiness area to include elementary and middle school students along with our high school and college students. We found a remarkably talented and dedicated roster of indigenous com-munity partners. This built democratic leadership across the entire spectrum of the partnership.

In an age of acute institutional stress, what remains is making the case for the fiscal, educational, and public benefits of these partnerships. We turn to this in the next chapter.

Notes

1. Richard Guarasci and David Mapstone, "Intercultural Citizenship and Democratic Sensibility at Hobart and William Smith Colleges," in *To Serve and Learn*, ed. Joseph L. DeVitis, Robert W. Johns, and Douglas J. Simpson (New York: Peter Lang Publishers, 1998), 61.

2. John Dewey, *Democracy and Education* (New York: Macmillan, 1916), 87.

3. Richard Guarasci, "On the Challenge of Becoming the Good College," *Liberal Education* 92, no. 3 (Winter 2006); see also "Transforming Undergraduate Education," an Interview with Richard Guarasci, *Peer Review*, Summer/Fall 2001.

4. For a very early approach that I found foundational, see Carole Pateman, *Participation and Democratic Theory* (Cambridge, UK: Cambridge University Press, 1975).

5. William Sullivan, *Work and Integrity: The Crisis and Promise of Professionalism in America* (New York: Harper Collins, 1995).

6. C. P. Snow, *The Two Cultures and the Scientific Revolution* (Cambridge, UK: Cambridge University Press, 1959).

7. Donald Schon, *The Reflective Practitioner* (New York: Basic Books, 1983); see also Donald Schon, *Educating the Reflective Practitioner* (San Francisco: Jossey-Bass, 1997).

5

MAKING THE CASE
FOR NEIGHBORHOOD
PARTNERSHIPS

Higher education has been confronted by three simultaneous pandemics. First, colleges and universities are entangled in an unremitting worldwide health crisis that not only challenges the health and safety of students, faculty, staff, and the entire neighboring community but also casts a shadow across the very existence of those institutions that suffer from their own underlying fiscal decline. Ominously, a number of health experts forecast a series of such health pandemics in future decades. Second, the political economy of higher education is predicated on a seriously flawed business model that threatens many universities and colleges. Finally, the exploding resistance to the political, economic, and social injustice of systemic racism and its parent, the residue of White supremacy, will challenge the legacies and operations of today's higher education institutions. This will demand serious campus changes.

In the face of these epic challenges, how and why should universities and colleges sustain comprehensive civic engagement commitments? How can they afford them? Wouldn't they appear to institutional leaders and stakeholders as untenable luxuries in an era of fiscal retreat? This chapter will make the case for the fiscal, educational, and reputational benefits of comprehensive anchor partnerships for universities and their neighboring communities. The first part of the chapter chronicles the best case for these partnerships and some of the key obstacles to success. The second part explores the Wagner College-PRP in depth.

The Benefits of Anchor Neighborhood Partnerships

Comprehensive university-neighborhood partnerships hold the potential for fiscal, educational, reputational, philanthropic, economic, and political benefits. To realize them, leaders must be visionary, practical, resilient, and persistent. Designing, building, and administering anchor partnerships require not only resources and inclusive decision-making but also democratic sensibilities and diplomatic patience. In short, the arts of democracy are just as essential for leaders of anchor partnerships as they are for educating students for democratic engagement. Both require critical thinking, active listening, the development of a clearly articulated vision and voice, much empathy and reciprocity, and the skills of building inclusive coalitions for designing and implementing solutions to numerous challenges. At their base, these partnerships are fortified by mutual respect and personal trust. Positive interpersonal relationships are absolutely critical for their productivity and ultimate success.

For the universities and colleges, the return on investment crosses all sectors of the campus.[1] When conducted successfully, these institutions will see gains in student learning and fiscal performance. In addition, participating faculty members will realize a variety of benefits. Academic and administrative offices will find greater opportunities for productive collaboration while the areas of equity and inclusion can have significant advances. And, not to be dismissed, universities and colleges will find a clarity of mission and focus with the campus community and the public.

Neighborhood partners have much to gain as well. They realize access to educational, research, and physical resources as well as direct services in areas of significant inequalities. In addition, the community partners achieve greater economic and community development opportunities. Most important, the local community develops a significant ally in its relationships with a host of governmental, political, and civic agencies. Overall, a successful partnership creates an intimacy that forges a mutuality elevating the identity, self-esteem, and voice of both the university and the neighborhood.

Student Learning

As I argued in chapter 4, engagement is the key to learning. Experiential learning allows students to associate the classroom with real issues and challenges, connecting "texts and experience." Learning occurs through the process of student reflection, where interpretation and meaning are made. With engaged civic learning, students connect the substance of the course texts and classroom sessions with the realities of these subjects as they unfold in everyday life.

First, I offer a qualitative case. In my own teaching, I have witnessed the remarkable learning that students have accomplished. In the previous chapter, I presented Kendra's deep reflection on her civic experience. What I didn't offer was the depth of her analysis of the course readings as she connected and contrasted each of them with her field experience. Without a doubt, she garnered a much greater understanding of the authors and their arguments about diversity, American democracy, personal identity, and inequality. I always ask my students to read competing positions on the course topics. They can easily settle for comfort in those that confirm their personal perspectives. I want them to encounter these authors and their arguments and compare them to what they observe in the community. I want them to ask key questions of the communities where they are working.

Another illustration of the power of civic engaged learning comes from the course I taught in the First Year Program (FYP) at Wagner College in 1998. As part of a learning community of twenty-four students, my course, Democracy and Diversity, was paired with Introduction to American Literature.[2] In addition, students were sorted into appropriate community placements with agencies and organizations whose work was deeply embedded into the work of diversity, equality, and social justice. This third course in the LC was called a "reflective tutorial" where students would draw from the content of the two disciplinary courses, political science and English, in reflecting on and writing about the interplay of their civic field experience informed by their course authors and texts.

In my course, we read a wide variety of pieces ranging from the foundational documents of American government and critical pieces on American domestic policy to essential essays and books on race, gender, and class in the United States. These included works by Audre Lorde, Arthur Schlesinger, Robert Coles, Cornel West, and Gloria Anzaldua. Students also read a generative and comprehensive history of immigration to the United States over its two hundred years, *A Different Mirror: A History of Multicultural America*, written by the late Ronald Takaki.[3] He examined how different ethnic and racial groups fared as immigrants in the United States from the eighteenth to the twentieth century. Among the groups Takaki studied were immigrants from Africa, China, Japan, Ireland, Germany, Italy, Mexico, and several other nations. Twinning the two disciplinary courses with the exact same students allowed for a pedagogical elegance where students would be studying and discussing the history of one particular ethnic group in my political science course while reading the literary fiction of, by, and about the same group in the English class. This allowed for a deep immersion around the themes, tensions, and challenges within and around diversity and American democracy.

We placed our learning community students with nonprofit organizations in the neighborhoods of newer New York City immigrants from Mexico, the Dominican Republic, Haiti, Central America, and Liberia. We also placed some students with the Staten Island AIDS Task Force and others at Ellis Island Museum, where the history of immigration was portrayed to the general public. This field work allows for very intense discussions around race, gender, and class issues both in the present time and in retrospect. Throughout the semester, students examined the promise and pitfalls of American democracy. The field experience offered a valuable granularity most often missing from more typical seat-time learning.

Here is the rub. Probably the most dedicated and sincere freshman student in that learning community unwittingly demonstrated civic learning's critical value added. Michelle was everything a teacher would seek in a first-year student, namely open to learning, questioning the course materials, and working hard to make meaning of the course. Her reactions were somewhat of a surprise during a daylong class trip to Williamsburg, then a fast-gentrifying community in Brooklyn. We exposed our students to the ethnic richness and complexity of this neighborhood where African Americans, Puerto Ricans, Italian Americans, and Hasidic Jews lived. It has always been a diverse neighborhood, dating to the days when my Sicilian immigrant grandparents raised my father and my aunts in a very modest attached tenement. In 1998, Williamsburg was in the midst of a dramatic, unexpected, and somewhat antagonistic process of White gentrification. Then and now, new immigrants populated New York City. They fuel the city's economic growth and cultural dynamism. Fifty percent of all children born in New York City have mothers who were not born in the United States. Michelle learned all of this in our courses. She was well prepared for our field trip where we wanted our students to grapple with the struggle to achieve economic growth and neighborhood enhancement while promoting racial and ethnic justice for long-ignored groups that are held down on the socioeconomic ladder by market forces. While this is asking much from first-semester students, it is, after all, the point of the entire freshman learning community. The students are now in college and are facing the objective challenges for their generation. Welcome to the world.

We spent the morning in the Hasidic neighborhood. Our hosts were very explicit about their goals to build homes to last centuries and to have very large families fill up the neighborhood. Most of these residents emigrated from Israel, believing it to be too secular for their understanding of Judaism. They were replacing old and worn wooden homes with new and impressive brick ones.

We next spent time with the declining but resilient Italian American section of Williamsburg. The residents were proud, not moving out, determined to benefit from the city's renaissance but wary of the real estate ambition of the new Israeli population. After this discussion and lunch, we moved to the Puerto Rican and African American sections of the community. Residents were just recovering from the merciless violence and destruction of the crack cocaine decade of the 1980s. Unlike the Italian and Jewish sections, all of the residents in these neighborhoods were renters. When exiting the van at one stop in this part of the neighborhood, my students thought that they encountered a dead bunny at the curb only to be told by those more familiar with urban realities that the "bunny" was a large dead rat, not an anomaly on these streets. After hanging on through the drug wars, these residents now were under siege from developers and landlords who were raising their rents rather dramatically in an effort to push them out and benefit from the emerging gentrification.

Our last stop was the gentrified section that looked like the neighborhood from the popular television show *Friends*. We left the troubles of the last section as we turned the corner and found an explosion of retail establishments, including Starbucks, Bed Bath & Beyond, artisan bakeries, and new age furniture stores. At this moment, Michelle, a first-generation four-year college student, turned to me and said, "President Guarasci, I hope when I graduate that I can live in a neighborhood like this section of Williamsburg." It was a golden opportunity for a teachable moment where those generative course readings and her field experience met the realities on the ground. I responded with a gentle question about one or another of the readings on inequality and then probed about the field experience as well. I then said that my hope for her was that her Wagner education would allow her to flourish in her chosen profession. I presented her with a new dilemma. How would she fulfill her rightful dream for an adult life in a culturally nourishing neighborhood while avoiding costing the Puerto Rican and African American renters their homes as landlords made room for new apartments, co-ops, and condos that would price them out? Wouldn't this relegate them to some other part of the city or its surrounding segregated areas?

I suspect that Michelle would not be different from many of our students who wanted to see social justice achieved through greater opportunities and more resources available to underserved populations. She wanted to be part of a more equitable and nonracist America. But like most of her classmates, she was compartmentalizing her personal life from the larger impersonal menu of political and economic choices embedded in American urban realities. As she reflected on all of this, she had a much deeper understanding of our readings, the course themes, and the dilemmas of working through the difficulties in finding a pathway that marries economic growth and social justice. I can say with some confidence that the combination of twinned courses and a common cohort of students joined with meaningful civic engagement allowed for much greater engagement, reflection, and knowledge than the seat time in my counterpart courses.

This portrait presents a qualitative example of the power of civic learning through a set of courses in community-based learning. In the main, the quantitative studies on the efficacy of civic learning demonstrate very real impacts. The respective research works of Alexander Astin and Linda Sax, Sylvia Hurtado, and several others demonstrate the positive impact as measured by traditional academic indicators.[4] The overall direction points to students who are engaged in courses with civic experiences achieving higher grade point averages and persisting to the degree. In particular, first-generation students graduate from four-year colleges and attend graduate school in greater numbers. My personal qualifier to these data is that such courses and experiences must be done responsibly, with the teaching faculty carefully cultivating deep reflection through a complete integration of the field work into class discussions and complementing the course readings. My previous comments on the limits of community-based learning still pertain. These are semester experiences and not transformational for the neighborhood community. But insofar as we privilege quantitative traditional measures of learning outcomes, the data demonstrate the value added of civic experience for student achievement in learning.

When involved in civic work, students also benefit to a greater degree from increased self-esteem. The research of psychologist Corey Keyes provides rich data on the impact of such activities on student flourishing.[5] Essentially, civically engaged students who focus on the needs of others have a greater sense of belonging and higher self-regard. Students realize that they matter to others. The research and educational work of the higher educational association Bringing Theory to Practice has highlighted much of these findings. The organization has provided hundreds of small but helpful grants to colleges that integrate civic work as an important element in reducing barriers to undergraduate learning. In my own teaching and leadership of civic work, and particularly in neighborhood partnerships, I have witnessed numerous students who previously were underachieving and feeling disconnected from college learning find measurable academic success and personal well-being.

At Wagner, as part of the PRP, there were a number of distinct examples of these results. A number of them were African American males who came to the college as NCAA athletes. They found great personal satisfaction in mentoring students in Port Richmond and the bordering areas. These young teens were on a clear path along the school-to-prison pipeline, but my Wagner students were a mystery to them. Someone who looked like them, who was bigger, stronger, and a better athlete, somehow was a successful college student. They would ask, "How did you do it. Isn't college just for White kids?" After a semester or a summer tutoring these youngsters, the Wagner students would return to campus with greater self-confidence. They were heroes in Port Richmond and now more sure of themselves on campus. Suddenly they found more pride and purpose in their undergraduate education. Their civic work opened a door for them. One male student, Jared, came to Wagner as a highly talented athlete who suffered from learning disabilities, manifested by a pronounced stutter. He barely made it through the first semester and immediately was on academic probation. Jared found his way into civic and inclusion work, mostly in the PRP, and by his senior year, he was giving public speeches, leading significant campus civic work, and achieving respectable academic outcomes. Today he is a successful high school teacher. The civic work was a bridge that gave him purpose and perseverance. At Wagner, this is one of so many examples of significant student self-esteem derived from civic work that spanned all types of students across the socioeconomic spectrum and the academic skill sets they had when entering college.

The previously cited research findings of Sylvia Hurtado and the others cited in her work point to the discernible mutual impact of civic experience, community-based learning, and interculturalism.[6] Civically engaged students gain meaningful experiences in collaborating with others different from themselves through civic work. Too often, university students mirror the residential segregation that is modern day America. Whoever they are in ethnicity, race, gender, class, and other identities, they all arrive to campus as if they were immigrants to the shores of an unknown nation. The current social geography does not prepare them for learning and living across these divides. They bring with them subtle biases, assumptions, and anxieties produced by years of segregated living. Without intentional educational practices, they could easily leave college with all of this baggage reinforced. Intentional diversity, inclusion, and civic engagement placed inside the curriculum, as well as throughout the campus cocurriculum, and with the neighborhood community, increase the probability that students are more capable of understanding the social forces that have resulted in an inequitable and segregated America. When immersed in civic work with community partners around the reduction of these conditions through practical community work, students begin the project of educational, psychological, and political reconstruction that is critical for the dawn of transformative leadership for meaningful social change. They begin learning the arts of democracy as tools for building a just and dynamic democracy. Some of these traits are discernible in the research, as in this finding by Sylvia Hurtado: "these studies show evidence regarding the link between diversity and civic minded practice on the one hand and student educational outcomes on the other."[7]

One example from Wagner's PRP is particularly illustrative. I worked with Patti Anne when she was a first-year student in my seminar on great thinkers. She is a White middle-class student from the suburbs. She was full of idealism and willing to take intellectual challenges. I rediscovered her as a sophomore when she became fully engaged with the educational pipeline work in the PRP. I would doubt that she had ever spent any significant time in a diverse, poor, and working-class community like Port Richmond. I watched her transformation from an innocent young woman, absent any significant experience with racial and ethnic diversity. She was new to this type of sustained civic work as well. She likely did volunteer work in high school as isolated community service. I would not have predicted how deeply committed she became to this community. She was a very valued person to the Mexican community, growing socially and intellectually from what this community taught her. She gained so much confidence.

By her senior year, Patti was running a major program with one of our local elementary schools where she began every school day there at 7 a.m. to make sure that all her children and many of their non-English-speaking parents were present. She tutored both children and parents. Her ability to hear the authentic lived experience of these somewhat endangered yet resilient families changed Patti. I watched her grow in her abilities in building emphatic and reciprocal relationships. She found ways to build solutions to everyday challenges that are a constant currency in Port Richmond. She became an engaged learner and an active agent for civic justice. Moreover, she was developing as a transformational leader. She graduated from Wagner, joined Teach for America, completed a master's degree along the way, and now is back in her suburban community as a teacher and, most importantly, as a civic professional. I could name another two dozen students from Patti's first year at Wagner who followed this path.

The data and my personal experience support the genuine impact of civic work, community-based learning, and, most acutely, sustained multiyear civic work in a neighborhood partnership, all leading to increased academic learning and academic success as measured in course grades, student persistence, and degree completion. They enhance self-esteem and confidence, social purpose, intercultural understanding, the importance of ethnic and racial justice, and, finally, significant competence through the acquisition of the arts of democracy.

Fiscal and Institutional Benefits

The national data previously cited support the assertion that civic engagement increases student retention. Clearly, this is an important element in helping students become successful learners and persist in enrollment. Ultimately, civic engagement leads to degree completion. The financial impact for colleges and universities is increased enrollment and, consequently, increased gross tuition revenue. This should result in an increase in net tuition revenue.

Student retention, coupled with the complementary increase in net revenue, is the fastest way for colleges to enhance their operating resources. It takes longer to grow net revenue from endowment increases because university endowment spending rates are usually capped at 5 percent. Increases in student retention almost always have a larger rate of incremental net revenue. For instance, hypothetically retaining a student instead of losing a student would mean, on average, a savings of 50 percent (at a 50 percent discount rate) of gross tuition or, on average, approximately $20,000. To earn this same amount annually from an endowment gift, which only allows a draw of 5 percent or less, would require a gift of $400,000.

To fully realize the financial elasticity of student retention, saving one student from dropping out is far more impactful in the immediate sense than the likely prospect of matching every student who potentially leaves with an additional $400,000 gift from a donor. From this perspective, the financial power from any of the student success strategies that prove effective will result in significant fiscal gains for the college or university. One of the best student retention strategies is engaged civic learning, which is a foundational curricular and cocurricular piece of any anchor partnership. This is an essential aspect of the financial case for civic engagement and civic partnerships.

The lesson learned from the advantage of civic work is a pedagogical theorem I like to flaunt when meeting with skeptical donors, business officers, directors, trustees, and faculty members. Namely, good educational practice will increase net tuition revenue. I should call it Guarasci's iron law of civic prosperity. Once, when I was asked to speak at a major national meeting of higher education business officers and academic deans, I couldn't deny myself a delicious moment in trotting out this educational gem. We were assembled in a large hotel in Washington DC, on a cold winter day. I was going to be the first speaker on the early opening panel. The audience gathered slowly. Before we started, I noticed that the nattily dressed members, likely the college business officers, were all reading the *Wall Street Journal* while finishing that last cup of morning coffee. The less sartorially attired were likely the college academic officers and they were checking their phones. Instinctively, I knew that to get the attention of this audience at this ungodly morning hour I needed to be bold and loud. So, after the expected introduction, which by the way did little to gain the interest of the CFOs, I bellowed out, "This presentation is about how good educational practice will increase your institution's net tuition revenue!" With that, every one of the business officers closed up their *Wall Street Journals*. The magnetism of money does compel the minds of those responsible for managing it. I hit a nerve. Point made.

Civic work and anchor partnerships in particular promise other financial benefits. First and foremost is the increase in philanthropic gifts and grants. Anchor partnerships that attack racial and ethnic inequality, increase degree completion in high school and college, and nurture civic leadership are in demand at almost all of the major philanthropies that fund higher education. The increment in this type of support will add significant resources for civic initiatives.

The number of individual donor prospects interested in meaningful, nonpartisan civic and anchor initiatives is not insignificant. The movement to end the school-prison pipeline, and now the acceptance and adoption of the goals of Black Lives Matter, all point to the imperative need to enhance philanthropic support to address institutional racism. To launch a partnership, universities need go no further than the doorstep of America's de facto apartheid educational system in confronting these issues.

Civic engagement programs generate significant foundation grants and individual philanthropic donations. With the increased focus on the social impacts of civic and anchor work, universities have the opportunity to excite their traditional annual fund donors, who largely consist of alumni, parents, and friends of the institution. This work will excite the imaginations and affiliations of those stakeholders. Different from endowment giving, which adds to the capital investment fund of the college, annual funds are almost always direct contributions to institutional operating funds and programmatic budgets. They are additions to annual spending. Similar to fiscal gains derived from student retention, annual funds produce immediate fiscal enhancements while endowment funds protect the long-standing fiscal health of the university but are only spent at 5 percent of value in any given year. They offer less immediate assistance but provide long-term security.

One additional development asset is planned giving. The contributions are drawn from wills, estates, and the like. This is a very promising arena for civic support, because those with moderate means can plan on leaving parts of their estate to provide support for civic commitments. This donor base is not limited to prospects with extraordinary assets, because it cuts across a much wider spectrum of donors who have more tempered, but cumulatively significant financial capacity.

In my experience at Wagner, I inherited an underfunded institution with almost a negligible endowment and nine times that amount in bonded debt. For its short history, founded as a college in 1929, it had a small and somewhat modest wealth index for its alumni. Yet with all these inhibitors, the endowment increased from $4 million to $98 million in my seventeen years at the college, and the debt stabilized around the inherited amount of approximately $50 million.[8] Moreover, the annual budget for Wagner in my last years as president averaged around $120 million, and through grants and gifts we were averaging approximately $325,000 in direct support and another $50,000 in kind as externally funded staff for our Center for Leadership and Community Engagement.

There are two other areas of institutional advancement opportunities for comprehensive anchor partnership. The first is the palpable impact on the university's reputation and identity both locally and nationally. Becoming a leader in this work has benefited many anchor partners through the educational, social, and civic impact. Higher education ranking systems such as *U.S. News & World Report*, Campus Compact, and the American Council of Education recognize these efforts, and a number of other national associations provide annual recognitions. In addition, the agencies that govern the required institutional accreditation include civic engagement as a key component in their respective criteria. Gaining recognition as a civically engaged college or university is a highly competitive recognition that is vetted through a thorough and demanding process under the auspices of the Carnegie Foundation. Philanthropic organizations and foundations seek out this designation when making grants. Locally, there are numerous local recognitions for this important work. It becomes a matter of community and university pride as well as a significant badge with the relevant local and state agencies and elected officials.

In addition to this type of institutional praise, the impact on the campuses of a number of universities and colleges has been immense. This helps to galvanize institutions that may be internally diffuse, as was the case at Portland State University in the 1990s. The new president, Judith Ramaley, was confronted by an urban university that appeared as a holding company comprising a variety of schools and programs seemingly disconnected from one another. She looked for a common identity that would give the university a unifying common mission. Part of her plan included a comprehensive reform of the undergraduate general education requirements, accompanied by a full-blown civic engagement dimension involving civic learning and community partnerships. Her elegant refrain to create an identity for the educational program was "let knowledge serve the city." From that simple tagline, President Ramaley framed remarkable and nationally celebrated civic and educational initiatives that vaulted Portland State into the mainstream of innovative universities. It became a national educational leader and a prime example of the impact of civically engaged institutions. Previously, Portland State was an obscure regional institution. The university began to realize major foundation grants in large amounts and garnered greater respect among legislative leaders.

Another benefit of civic partnerships is the impact on the participating faculty members. The civic mission provides a clear focus for them. It often aligns their teaching and research agenda through a continuing commitment to engaging and solving community challenges, most of which touch on issues of inequality. I have observed that engaged Wagner College faculty found this work quite rewarding. It didn't matter what discipline was involved. It ranged from scientists teaching and researching around environmental challenges or art history faculty finding a way to engage young elementary and middle school students around perception, ways of seeing, and critical thinking. Often, the latter would open up new vistas for children in neighborhood schools where the arts are absent, and these students would deploy the various arts in expressing the everyday challenges in their community. Of course, the applied disciplines and social sciences were natural fits in linking teaching, scholarship, and community needs. Through debates and other pedagogical methods, even fields such as philosophy and literature found innovative means to help youngsters engage serious issues that were considered too difficult for them to comprehend. Often, ethics and justice issues and definitions of citizenship would become prime subjects for middle and high school students in Port Richmond. These types of alignments produced a score of articles in academic journals, as well as a number of books.

The civic work becomes problem-based teaching. The community identifies its needs and priorities in a democratically organized partnership. Engaging college students in these types of efforts gives them a sense of control or personal agency in directing their own education. Most often, this type of problem-based learning involves an interdisciplinary approach. Problems present themselves in real time in real places. They require a variety of skills and disciplines to fully engage them. Apart from the obvious learning benefits for students, faculty members collaborate across the academic departments and disciplines, significantly increasing their productivity. A unified faculty is a major benefit to a successful university or college. Finding common and meaningful purpose almost always increases productivity and innovation.

Finally, the civic partnerships open up the opportunity for critical dialogues around race, class, and gender, as well as economic inequality within courses and across the campus. These conversations are rooted in the granularity of inequality, which is experienced every day within these neighborhoods. This allows the campus inequities of race and ethnicity to be vividly exposed, often leveling the playing field for minority students in confronting their White peers. The commitment to justice in the community creates a common expectation for civically engaged students, and that comes back to campus in the form of an interrogation of hidden and explicit biases formerly ignored. Interracial dialogues can provide much richer and honest personal and institutional analysis.

In the end, the central point to be made to those responsible for educational institutions is that civic commitments, particularly of the anchor model, are not a fiscal drain on the already deleted college treasuries. In fact, they can be self-sufficient, if not financially value added. They surely are a net asset for the campus community.

The Case for the Community

Anchor partnerships provide a large variety of benefits to the neighborhood and many of its residents. Depending on the type of partnership, these can be quite sizable. The largest partnerships involve major hospital systems, K–12 educational systems, and significant university employment and real estate interests. We will examine some of these different models in chapter 6.

The partnership affects the neighborhood community in a number of meaningful ways. Among them are improved educational opportunities, greater health-care resources, economic advancement, greater business development and local employment, elevated neighborhood pride, and increased neighborhood leadership capacity. In addition, these anchor partnerships often unite dispersed and sometimes competing leaders and institutions within shadow neighborhoods.

The educational gains are numerous. Focusing on preparing students for college readiness in the early elementary grades underwrites higher education as an expectation as opposed to a fantasy for these youngsters. This one element alone is revolutionary in communities with underperforming and troubled schools. The college readiness approach unites parents, children, schoolteachers, and administrators with college faculty, administrators, and university students. They enhance literacy programs and reading and math initiatives through tutoring, better classroom management through additional college-provided staffing, and after-school programs featuring greater academic, cocurricular, and athletic programming. In neighborhoods like Port Richmond, partnerships provide critical literacy initiatives for parents and children. As I noted in chapter 1, students who are significantly behind in reading by the fourth grade have a highly reduced chance of graduating high school, never mind gaining entrance to college. These additional educational assets provided by the college or university can reverse the fate of so many children who otherwise would find themselves in the teeth of the school-to-prison pipeline.

Again, I turn to Wes Moore to vividly illustrate what that looks like. In his most recent book, *Five Days*, Wes Moore and Erica Green chronicle the five days in Baltimore surrounding the killing of the late and young Freddie Gray, another victim of unaccountable police brutality against a Black man, for little to no cause.[9] Without describing the account of those events here, the critical point that underscores the imperative of an educational pipeline partnership between universities and shadow neighborhoods is that Fred Gray was a victim of an economic, political, and social system of sustained racial subordination and intergenerational poverty.

As Moore argues, Freddie almost was destined to have an unjust and brutal end. He was born to a heroin-addicted mother, which resulted in months in detox as a newborn. He came home to a lead-filled apartment. The impact of lead on cognitive development is well documented. He fell well behind in school in the early grades, became a behavior problem for his teachers, and spent most of his time out of classrooms. He turned to the street economy as a drug runner at an early age, left high school, and started on the short road to crime, violence, and then the awful fate of police abuse and murder. What if Freddie Gray had been included in an intense reading and tutoring program in pre-K and through the elementary years? What if that program introduced him to college students who looked like him? What if this program emphasized community engagement and leadership development? What if this program began to teach Freddie how to articulate and advocate for his community? What if he made it through high school and college? What would that Freddie Gray offer to his community and to the entire Baltimore community? What would he provide to the national movements for interracial democracy, economic justice, and civic prosperity? What if that Freddie Gray were alive today?

Since underfunding for college guidance dramatically limits secondary schools, another benefit for K–12 partners is the opportunity to educate students and families about college. University admissions offices and their student volunteers fill this gap. I have seen high schools with five hundred or more students have only one guidance counselor. College counseling was just one of many functions for that position.

The college readiness focus of the partnerships provides access to campus facilities. This can be critical in so many ways. For poor children and families, college campuses are unknown and somewhat feared locations. These individuals often feel they don't belong, and they would be unwelcome. Simply inviting them onto campuses, often accompanied by their college student tutors, demystifies "college."

One searing example that I witnessed at Wagner occurred during a college tour program we set up for all freshman students at a PRHS. This was in the early years. Since then, both elementary and middle school students have had regular campus visits. In this initial year, we presented almost a full day of programs that ranged from why college is necessary to how to afford it to how to apply and how to prepare oneself for acceptance to the full range of colleges. Students heard from the president and all the major academic administrators as well as a number of college students. After lunch in the main dining room with the usual undergraduate and graduate students, the high school freshmen, many from formerly rural Mexican families, received a campus tour from the student guides. After a review of science labs, classrooms, the theater facilities, nursing and health sciences resources, and athletic facilities, these youngsters, daunted by these somewhat opulent college surroundings, would ask their college guides, "You live here? Where do the parents live on campus?" This college world was so dramatically different from anything they could have imagined. When told they could reside on campus if they chose, but no one's parents lived on a college campus, they were learning that college life expected them to be in charge of their everyday life.

The students' innocence demonstrated the value of simply opening up the campus and welcoming them. A psychological wall was taken down. The more they came to campus for any number of academic and related programs, the more likely they were to see college as attainable, permissible, and expected. I might add that these types of encounters made enduring impacts on the college community's understanding of and commitment to Port Richmond.

Partnerships provide direct service benefits to the community. Those partnerships that involve health-care institutions usually have direct service commitments from medical schools, nursing and physician assistant programs, and all the related health sciences. These take many forms, including accentuating required student field placements into the neighborhood community's hospitals and health-care nonprofits. In addition, universities can provide volunteers for health screenings and basic workups. The ability to share facilities, research opportunities, expertise, and resources for health-care needs is demonstrated in a variety of ways previously unavailable in shadow neighborhoods, which are almost always underfunded.

Other program areas benefit through direct deployment of student interns, field placement, and directed research. This would include small business development through the assignment of accounting and finance students who are capable of preparing business plans, loan applications, preliminary tax statements, and related activities. Criminal justice majors offer all sorts of possibilities for courts and administrative offices that are overloaded and understaffed.

With larger universities, real estate assets can become major advances for the community. Rutgers University–Newark leads the way in assistance for repurposing abandoned or failing buildings and, along with other community partners, utilizing them as highly effective arts facilities for neighborhood artists, performers, and youth programs. In addition, university hiring and employment practices can be redirected to address the community's chronic unemployment while injecting more revenue into the neighborhood's local economy. And in this vein, college purchasing policies can be altered to favor and nurture neighborhood vendors in many areas, but particularly in food and supplies.

Before I turn to the PRP case study, I want to focus on two very important community macro opportunities from anchor partnerships. First, the impact on schools can be quite significant. Clearly, the focus is on children and adolescent learning, but there is also a powerful effect on administrators and teachers. These are schools without significant allies and advocates. The introduction of the university as a committed and resilient partner opens up all the previously cited benefits while providing an invaluable resource for K–12 teachers who tend to be underpaid, undersupported, and ignored. They are given a very difficult challenge, and by finding allies in the faculty from the schools of education and all the academic disciplines, they can prosper. Universities that provide guided career coaching and professional development above and beyond their postbaccalaureate degree programs will provide critical emotional, pedagogical, and career support. I witnessed such a program at Wagner where teacher retention grew from 50 percent to 90 percent over five years. These efforts are a key part of K–12 student success and need to be incorporated into any educational pipeline partnership.[10]

Second, the potential economic gains of a comprehensive partnership can be significant. Elevating the educational, aesthetic, and social assets in a poor, but now engaged community will interest those seeking investment opportunities. This can start with small business and can invite the attention of the local economic development corporations as government-supported coalitions of private business interests. Just supporting the local mom-and-pop enterprises increases the vitality and self-esteem of these neighborhoods. Larger enterprises take notice, particularly if local banks and government partners begin to play a positive and active role. After all, struggling communities have a pattern of suddenly becoming fashionable destinations for dining, retail, and cultural events. The trick is to guide this newfound economic momentum into a just economic outcome as opposed to the present version of gentrified relocation of the lower classes.

Finally, the significant increase in neighborhood identity and community pride is one of the major community benefits from anchor partnerships. I witnessed it in the Rust Belt town of Geneva, New York, in the 1990s and again on Staten Island's Port Richmond neighborhood in the past dozen years. I must add, however, that this newly gained self-confidence is contingent on the sustained commitment of the major anchor partners, particularly the college or university. Without that alliance, shadow neighborhoods can easily sink back into obscurity, ignored by the political, economic, and cultural authorities and reviving the narrative of the inevitability of inequality's permanence.

Institutional Expense for Civic Partnerships

Many, if not most, universities and colleges maintain civic engagement programs. A growing number are initiating or sustaining partnerships with their local communities. Having outlined the benefits to these institutions, the next critical question to be answered is: What should these commitments cost in annual operating expenses? Naturally, the size of the university and the scope of the anchor partnerships will vary accordingly, and therefore the expense outlays for anchor partnerships will differ. Institutions with substantive civic engagement programs usually maintain manageable budgets to support their work. These expenditures usually include an office, staff, and budget for operations. Introducing a partnership will add cost, the size of which will vary with the scope of the commitment. Does the college support civically engaged courses within the curriculum? Are these offered across the curriculum? Does the student affairs office support extensive civic engagement opportunities throughout the cocurriculum? Does the institution manage these programs with a dedicated office or center for civic engagement? If the answers to these questions are affirmative, then the costs of adding a partnership will be marginal, since a good deal of the needed infrastructure already is in place. If not, then the cost of initiating a partnership will be higher.

To better assess the expense impact, I will project a typical case for a small institution. The utility of this approach will allow for projections appropriate for different institutional types, sizes, and commitments. In my hypothetical model, I am assuming an institution with a student body of approximately 2,000 full-time equivalency (FTE), a gross revenue annual budget of $120 million, and an endowment of $100 million. These macro statistics generate an approximate gross spending per student of $6,000 and endowment per student at $5,000. One caveat: Endowments are not free to dedicate their full value purely to the academic functions of the college. Gifts are often tied to donor designations and support for physical campus assets. That caveat aside, these macro statistics offer operating metrics that allow for reviewing the costs of civic engagement and university partnerships as compared with the normal costs per student.

In my projected model, the annual operating costs for the entire civic engagement program and anchor partnership are estimated between $900,000 and $1 million in total. This accounts for the following expenses:

Projected Annual Operating Costs

1. Center for Civic Engagement..............................$645,000
   Director..$75,000
   Associate Director....................................$60,000
   Assistant Director....................................$45,000
   Administrative Assistant..............................$40,000
   Employee Benefits @ 28% = $75,000
   Budget..$50,000
   Bonner Scholars....................$150,000 (50 × $3,000)
   Transportation costs.................................$150,000
2. Additional Anchor Partnership Costs....................$253,000
   Three entry-level staff @ $40,000 each...............$120,000
   Employee benefits.....................................$33,000
   Summer program mentors................................$30,000
   Faculty support and stipends..........................$20,000
   Travel/transportation.................................$20,000
   Summer program meals..................................$20,000
   Miscellaneous/Discretionary funds.....................$10,000
3. Total Costs: Civic Engagement and Partnerships......$898,000
4. Discretionary Reserve.................................$100,000
5. Total Cost Ratios....Civic Engagement + Partnership = .075%
   of total college budget

   $$= \$450 \text{ per student FTE}$$
   $$= .009\% \text{ of endowment}$$

The appropriate civic engagement program costs, absent the partnership, are in excess of $600,000. This includes personnel salary costs for four staff, namely a director who oversees the program and works closely with faculty members and advancement staff to secure gifts and grants; an associate director who works directly with students, field placements, and community partners; an assistant director who works with civically engaged students and manages field placements; and an administrative assistant who supervises the office.

The partnership model also adds costs for an additional three staff members in the field and working with the major partner sites. For example, staff may be placed in the partner schools included in a K–12 pipeline program. Assuming a summer program for the high school students, a small corps of college students will serve as paid mentors. The summer program will require expenditures for daily lunch meals for the high school students, mentors, participating faculty instructors, and staff. I would assume transportation costs as well. In my model, I hold an approximate $100,000 in reserve for unexpected expenses for professional development and campus summer housing for the mentors, if needed.

The comparative ratios are sound metrics for demonstrating the total costs, representing an extremely low percentage of the college's gross operating revenue, less than 1 percent. The costs per student FTE throughout the college is totally in line with the traditional instructional ratio. All totals exclude any financial offsets from external funding such as grants and gifts. My experience would lead me to assume any reasonably competent and focused institutional advancement office would generate $200,000 to $400,000 in annual contributions from national, regional, and local foundations; major donors; annual fund donors; and alumni to support this program. This would reduce the impact on the annual operating budget by 20 to 40 percent. These comparative ratios drop significantly. In the end, this model demonstrates that a committed institution is able to manage the direct annual outlays within the normal confines of the annual budget and strategic goals. The only barriers to sustaining a comprehensive civic engagement program and neighborhood anchor partnership are not material but rather those related to values, dedication, and resiliency.

Case Study: The Wagner College-PRP

Introduction to Port Richmond and Wagner College

The Wagner College-PRP officially was founded in 2009. Preceding this date, the college president and a number of community leaders engaged in dialogue for several years. These meetings were listening sessions about several poor, racially segregated communities on Staten Island. Port Richmond stood out as a viable partner for Wagner College. It was a community of great need. It suffered from racial tensions. Many immigrants were undocumented, becoming victims of economic exploitation with little recourse due to their legal status. These families were hardworking, family-centered, and in real need of allies. The building of the partnership took time, patience, and determination to move all of these well-intentioned efforts to take hold. Once the process began, the college community and the neighborhood partners had a deeper understanding and appreciation of each other. But during the first decade of the twenty-first century, these two forces found each other through a steady march for mutual benefit.

Wagner College, a small, private, comprehensive liberal arts college, has been a presence on Staten Island since 1918 when it moved its high school Lutheran Seminary from Rochester, New York, with the ambition of becoming a four-year college. It achieved that goal in 1929 and immediately went coed in 1933. Even then, as a Lutheran institution, it professed to be open and welcoming to all regardless of faith, class, or race. Academic excellence and service to the larger community were engraved in its founding mission. This was largely expected to occur through the moral and academic teaching of its faculty, who in turn would help Wagner graduates develop and sustain these core values in their private and professional lives. Beyond charitable works, strategic and sustained civic engagement was not a formal dimension of the college.

In the other part of town, Port Richmond began as a Dutch Reform Church community around 1696. It became an independent village on Staten Island under the auspices of the Dutch colony and as the site of one of the first churches in New York State. It served as a transfer station for ferries to New Jersey. One of its historically significant native residents was Cornelius Vanderbilt, who would become one of the wealthiest Americans and the patriarch of a railroad dynasty in the nineteenth century.

Three hundred and fifty years from its origins, the neighborhood now known as Port Richmond blossomed to a population of more than 18,516 residents, as recorded by the U.S. census. Its home, Staten Island, is one of the five boroughs that constitute New York City. The borough has a population of approximately 500,000. Staten Island is larger than many American cities, such as St. Louis, Detroit, and Cleveland, but the borough is dwarfed by New York City's overall population of just under nine million residents. It regards itself as the "forgotten borough," ignored by the political and economic forces that distribute power and resources in the city.

Over its history, Port Richmond became home to a rich variety of ethnic communities, including many new immigrants to the United States. Today, it is home to a very large Mexican population, mostly from the State of Oaxaca in the country's southern region. On its face, this is a strange destination for

Mexican immigrants, given the more familiar landing points in California, Arizona, and Texas. In the northern section of Port Richmond, the population is heavily African American. This is a distressed community somewhat dispossessed politically on the island and overwhelmed by the dynamics of inequality. The groups have had a notable amount of racial tension. Finally, Port Richmond has a significant White working-class neighborhood that is perceived as a poor community beset by crime and violence. With some exceptions, Port Richmond is largely ignored or feared by the White residents of Staten Island, particularly the White enclave of the island's south shore, which faces New Jersey.

Overwhelmingly a borough with patches of Black and Brown communities found largely on the north shore facing back to Brooklyn and Manhattan, the Port Richmond neighborhood is one of Staten Island's shadow communities. Wagner College, on the other hand, is a source of local pride for its magnificent rise in the past twenty years as an innovative institution. It received national recognition for its unusual curriculum, The Wagner Plan for the Practical Liberal Arts, and for its commitment to comprehensive civic engagement embedded in its academic curriculum and its campus programs. In 1999, *Time* magazine selected the college as one of its Colleges of the Year in recognition of the Wagner Plan. In 2005, the American Council of Education awarded Wagner with the prestigious Theodore Hesburgh Award for its ambitious first-year program, and in 2009 it received national acclaim by President Bill Clinton and his foundation for what was then called the Port Richmond initiative.

As president, I was intent on moving Wagner's civic engagement efforts from the limits of semester-based projects to a more meaningful deployment of our student and faculty investment of time and labor into a strategic arrangement with a local community of need. The goal was to partner with a community and assist in helping it to shape its own civic, political, and economic fate. Simultaneously, the college would regain its civic mission and become a national civic leader. With that, I began searching for the appropriate community on Staten Island that would have a social infrastructure and indigenous leadership that would provide a long-term relationship. While Wagner would continue its civic commitments in all of these communities of need, we wanted to start an anchor partnership with a single neighborhood. For all the previously mentioned reasons about Port Richmond, I believed it held the most promise.

The partnership comprises approximately thirty community organizations that cut across a range of policy areas that were affirmed through a strategic planning process that involved Wagner College and the community. The community partners meet with the college leaders quarterly. The college president is a regular participant.

The Wagner Center for Leadership and Community Engagement was created to administer the civic engagement programs at the college. These include the field experience attached to the First-Year Program Learning Communities, which are required of all freshman students. It also directed all the field placements for the PRP work and all the field work of the students in the Bonner Leaders Program, which requires more than 300 hours per semester. In addition, the center assisted in field work placements associated with the senior learning communities, requiring more than 100 hours per student. The center did not, however, supervise all of the civic and prepro-fessional internships and practicums associated with the hundreds of hours required of the Nursing School, Physician Assistant, and Teacher Education programs each semester. For most of the past ten years, the center's director has reported to the president and provost.

The partnership is organized around five policy areas as illustrated in Figure 5.1. They include the arts and culture, economic development, college readiness, immigration and advocacy, and health and wellness.

A lead partner—an institutional as well as an individual leader—headed each area. In addition, each area had a major faculty and student facilita-tor. Overall, hundreds of students were engaged in partnership work in any given moment.

On the ground in Port Richmond, Wagner students tutored youngsters while college personnel provided guidance and mentoring for high school students, assisted with literacy initiatives, worked at and supervised food

Figure 5.1. PRP organization.

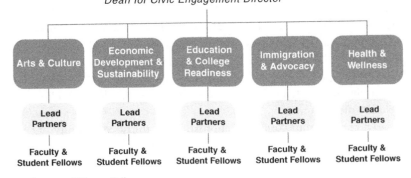

Source: Courtesy of Wagner College.

pantries and after-school academic and athletic activities, and created performances in the community with student and adult performers.

The Wagner College Educational Pipeline

To fully explain the extent of the partnership's impact, a few examples will detail the work. The college readiness programs became the most extensive and distinctive work of the partnership, which spawned a K–16 pipeline by establishing fully staffed college-school offices in elementary, middle, and high schools. The offices supported comprehensive programs for academic enrichment, leadership development, and civic engagement. The schools became feeders for one another so that youngsters in these schools, starting at around age ten in the fifth grade until senior year in high school at age eighteen, would be part of the school-to-college pipeline. The institutions worked together in coordinating the activities, and Wagner College staffed the K–12 school offices with professional coordinators and numerous college students as civic volunteers, most of whom were enrolled in Wagner's Bonner Leaders Program for civically engaged college students. Figure 5.2 sketches out the pipeline.

A number of elementary schools received Wagner students as mentors and tutors, but Public School 21 housed the College Awareness Office. Many of the school's graduates migrated to Intermediate School (IS) 51 for middle school and then a number of IS 51 graduates matriculated at Port Richmond

Figure 5.2. School-to-college pipeline.

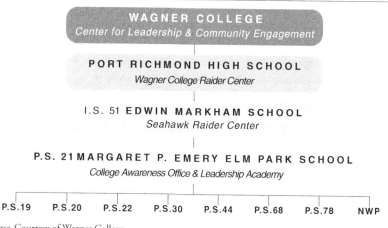

Wagner College Educational Pipeline

WAGNER COLLEGE
Center for Leadership & Community Engagement

PORT RICHMOND HIGH SCHOOL
Wagner College Raider Center

I.S. 51 EDWIN MARKHAM SCHOOL
Seahawk Raider Center

P.S. 21 MARGARET P. EMERY ELM PARK SCHOOL
College Awareness Office & Leadership Academy

P.S.19   P.S.20   P.S.22   P.S.30   P.S.44   P.S.68   P.S.78   NWP

Source. Courtesy of Wagner College.

High School. Each school had its Wagner College Center appropriately named with its school's mascot.

At the high school, first-year students with approximately a seventy-five to eighty-two average were eligible to apply for the Port Richmond Leadership Academy at Wagner College. The participating high school students immediately renamed our program "PRPLA." We did not aim for the highest scoring students because we believed they would find their way to college. Rather, we believed that the average student, who likely would not attend college, possessed the creative capacity for college entry and success if properly mentored in a program applying democratic pedagogical principles and practicing the arts of democracy. We began the program with generous funding initially from the New World Foundation and later from a very generous alumnus. After we were established, we received critical funding from the Charles Hayden Foundation as well as two private bank foundations on Staten Island.[11]

PRPLA is a three-year college readiness program that works through the Seahawk Raider Center at PRHS during the academic year and then migrates to a residential summer program on the Wagner campus. In the summer, students complete two enriched English and math or chemistry courses, plus a community-based learning seminar on the theory and practice of American democracy. This includes active civic engagement in their home neighborhood of Port Richmond with our community partners and supervised by Wagner students. In their junior and senior years, PRPLA high school students complete two regular Wagner College courses taught by full-time Wagner faculty members, usually in history, philosophy, and English. They also continue their civic internships in the community or in some cases at other more advanced opportunities outside Port Richmond. In the end, PRPLA students complete one semester of college as they graduate high school. In addition, Wagner offers full room, board, and tuition scholarships to at least four of the twelve students in each cohort year.

PRPLA began in 2013 with twelve rising sophomore students selected by the PRHS principal, Tim Gannon, and his staff in coordination with the staff of Wagner's Center for Leadership and Engagement. By 2016, all of the students completed high school. All of them were admitted to a college or university. Instead of four on full scholarship, Wagner admitted eight. The other four went to selective institutions. In 2020, all of them graduated from college. The Wagner eight, which included Mindy, who was introduced in chapter 1, all graduated and are Wagner alumni. Behind that class are three others. Only one student to date has not completed the PRPLA program.

After two years, Principal Gannon wanted his high school students to mirror the civic work of the Wagner students who were Bonner leaders.

He began to conceptualize a PRHS complement at IS 51 with its principal, Nick Mele. IS 51 is a feeder school to the high school. These PRHS students would pair up with the Wagner volunteers at IS 51. Later, the principal of elementary school 21, Anthony Cosentino, joined the work, and we established the center there. All of these principals are transformative educators, totally dedicated to their students' success and welfare and to the success of their respective faculty members. The college now formed a very tight circle of integrated leadership with the children and many parents in Port Richmond. For those students not formally in PRPLA, the Seahawk Raider Office became an important footprint for them as a place to learn about college, form friendships, and set higher goals for themselves.

A true educational community emerged among the schools and Wagner College. Students from all of the schools attended many athletic and academic events on the Wagner campus. These included special half-time recognition ceremonies for strong elementary school attendance and similar events for academic and civic excellence for the middle school students. We began a two-week summer program for IS 21 students on the Wagner campus, run by staff and Bonner leaders. Among other activities, these twelve- and thirteen-year-olds would write résumés and educational goal statements. Through a program underwriting the academic and civic principles of the arts of democracy, our mission was to demystify the college experience and prepare and support the students for college readiness and college success.

One example of the impact of this work is best told through the orientation and recognition ceremonies held each fall for PRPLA students and their families. On the eve of moving the PRPLA students into Wagner College residences, these high school sophomores and their families would gather for a special ceremony. Notably, many students arrived with many extended family members. This was a major moment for first-generation high school sophomores. They were moving onto a college campus for a few weeks. Many of their parents had never been on a college campus. After a number of welcoming speeches from the Wagner staff and Principal Gannon, we asked all of the family guardians to step forward and sign a pledge to support their children in this long journey to college. Then the students would sign the pledge. As they were about to leave the signing table at the front of the room, each family was given a globe representing their child's encounter with learning. We gave students handsome compasses and told them that no matter how hard the struggle, the compasses always pointed them toward college. Amid the tears of joy and hope by everyone in the room, it was a moment of determination and pride for the families, the PRPLA students, the Wagner students, the participating high school and Wagner faculty and staff, and many community partners.

Similarly, the year-end recognition ceremonies presented many awards in honor of academic, civic, and leadership achievements from the PRPLA students, Wagner students, and our partner community organizations. These were remarkable and indelible moments marking social change and interracial democracy.

The arts arena illustrated another example of the powerful impact of the partnership. Previously, the Port Richmond community was lacking in any meaningful way to register its voice about the everyday realities of life on its streets and in its homes. It was a place recently known for violence and crime. Prior to the partnership, conflicts erupted between African American and Mexican youth, both in the high school and on the streets. The major antipoverty organization on Staten Island, Project Hospitality, led by Reverend Terri Troia, began antiviolence initiatives. Members of the Wagner faculty and staff participated in these efforts. The partnership took inspiration from this work, and under its Arts and Culture banner, it started the Sounds of Port Richmond. Made up of local residents, PRHS students, and PRPLA and Wagner staff, a number of locally presented performances captured the issues most important to the community residents. One set of short pieces about episodes of interracial conflict was performed in both English and Spanish. At the end of each piece, as the actors stayed in character, the audience members were asked to speak to them, challenging their reactions to the various issues in the plays or suggesting additional characters. Keep in mind, however, that the "actors" were ordinary residents ranging from ten to seventy years old, and most were new to stage performance.

In the following years, the Sounds of Port Richmond would put on spectacular dance pieces around the refrain "we are Port Richmond," where the negative issues of domestic and street violence, bigotry, and racism would be contrasted with scenes of parental love and the joys of friendship. But the most moving performance took place after the murder of Eric Garner by police officers on a Staten Island street corner in broad daylight. This occurred down the block from Wagner College and not far from Port Richmond. Again, the performance was locally written by members of the partnership and first performed to amazingly large local audiences at the Staten Island Ferry Terminal. Later it was brought to local schools.

These are a few examples of the work of the Wagner College-PRP. To provide a fuller accounting would demand a book of its own. What should be evident is the rise of leadership and intercultural partnership among community residents, in the schools, among students, teachers and principals, college students and faculty members, artists and performers, and so many others. The pride and increased self-esteem among all these groups was palpable at all of these events. Students completed high school, successfully completed college, earned their undergraduate degrees, and began lives of meaning and public consequence. Wagner College coalesced in many ways around a civic purpose for its educational goals and ambitions. Its stakeholders and alumni, young and old, developed greater respect for the college.

The PRP is a good example of a comprehensive neighborhood commitment. Efficiently organized, it spawned leadership throughout the community and the campus. Students from a long-ignored community have gained important resources for college readiness. College students are engaged in learning the arts of democracy and better prepared to become civic professionals in their chosen careers. Wagner College has earned a reputation as a national leader in civic learning while Port Richmond has drawn more attention to its needs and found new confidence in meeting the challenges of an economically distressed community.

Nationally, these partnerships hold significant promise in addressing unremitting inequality and the enduring racial barriers. Without them, I wonder how higher education will overcome the dilemma of troubling demographics where the part of the college age population that is growing the largest will be the least able to afford it. Partnerships disrupt the school-prison pipeline, and they reduce, if not reverse, the impact of unsuccessful school systems on college-ready students. Morally, the civic imperative is ubiquitous. Society needs universities and colleges to become allies in addressing inequality as part of their historic civic mission. To achieve this goal, they must deepen their commitment to preparing a workforce for a dynamic and more equitable economy that must be led by educated and civically engaged citizens. Ultimately, the civic imperative for higher education is the only viable hope for restoring a university education as a public good and not merely limited as a private asset. Regaining the public trust is an essential element in restoring the health of higher education and, if done correctly, it will limit the damage of its seriously flawed business model, the parent of unaffordability and unsustainable student debt. Ultimately, the solution to this latter problem lies beyond the civic mission, but the road to reversing it may start with the civic commitment.

Notes

1. For a good introduction, see *Making Partnerships Work: Principles, Guidelines, and Advice for Public University Leaders* (Washington DC: American Association of State Colleges and Universities, 2017).

2. For a full description of this course and teaching experience, see Richard Guarasci, "The Wagner Plan for the Practical Liberal Arts: Deep Learning and Reflective Practice" in *Integrating Learning Communities with Service Learning*, ed. Jean MacGregor (Olympia, WA: National Communities Project, 2003), 23–29.

3. Ronald Takaki, *A Different Mirror: A History of Multicultural America* (New York: Little Brown, 1993).

4. Alexander Astin and Linda Sax, "How Undergraduates Are Affected by Service Participation," *Journal of College Student Development* 39, no. 3 (May–June 1998); Sylvia Hurtado and Linda DeAngelo, "Linking Diversity and Civic-Minded Practices with Student Outcomes: New Evidence from National Surveys," *Liberal Education* 98, no. 2 (Spring 2012); Dan Simonet, "Service Learning and Academic Success: The Links to Retention Research," Minnesota Campus Compact, 2008; Shauna Brazil, "Quantifying the Value of Service Learning: A Comparison of Grade Achievement between Service Learning and Non-Service-Learning Students," *International Journal of Teaching and Learning in Higher Education* 28, no. 2, 2016.

5. See C. Keyes and J. Haidt, eds., *Flourishing: Positive Psychology and the Life Well Lived* (Washington DC: American Psychological Association, 2003); see also Ziggi Ivan Santini, Charlotte Meilstrup, Carsten Hinrichsen, Line Nielsen, Ai Koyanagi, Steinar Krokstad, Corey Lee M. Keyes, and Vibeke Koushede, "Formal Volunteer Activity and Psychological Flourishing in Scandinavia," *Social Currents* 6, no. 3 (2019): 255–269.

6. Hurtado and DeAngelo, "Linking Diversity and Civic-Minded Practices," 2012; see also Mark E. Enberg and Sylvia Hurtado, "Developing Pluralistic Skills and Dispositions in College," *Journal of Higher Education* 82, no. 4 (2011): 416–443.

7. Hurtado and DeAngelo, "Linking Diversity and Civic-Minded Practices," 2012; see also Enberg and Hurtado, "Developing Pluralistic Skills and Dispositions in College," 2011, 416–443.

8. See Audited Financial Statements of Wagner College in 2002 and 2019, available from Wagner College and confirmed in the 2002 and 2019 IRS 990 fillings, available online.

9. Wes Moore and Erica Greene, *Five Days: The Fiery Reckoning of an American City* (New York: One Word Publishing, 2020).

10. For a full review of the New Educators at Wagner College Program, see Carin Guarasci's "When the Going Gets Tough: New Teachers' Perceptions of Emotional Intelligence Skills and Grit While Participating in a Support Program" (EdD diss., Teachers College, Columbia University, 2017).

11. Note the three Staten Island Bank Foundations that contributed to the funding of the Wagner College-PRP: The Richmond County Savings Bank Foundation, The Northfield Bank Foundation, and the Staten Island Foundation.

6

MODELS OF UNIVERSITY-NEIGHBORHOOD PARTNERSHIPS

In the past decade, many universities have moved to some form of community partnerships, including a vast array of arrangements. Historically, universities have been involved in place-based engagement since the birth of land grant universities after the Civil War and subsequently with their extension programs around agricultural improvements. Today's urban partnerships range from providing local schools with college preparedness programs to entrepreneurial agreements for shared services with local nonacademic institutions. Some of them are civic in nature while others are simply based on mutual fiscal advantages. As beneficial as these ventures may be, many are not comprehensive partnerships that address the deep inequalities found in their neighboring communities. I would refer to these types of partnerships as entrepreneurial as opposed to the focus of this book: transformative university-neighborhood partnerships.

In July 2019, *The Chronicle of Higher Education* issued its major report on the burgeoning business of university support for local communities. Titled *The Campus as City,*" the report describes a vast number of initiatives underway across America.[1] Many are joint public and private undertakings for local improvement. Some aim to reduce racial and class inequalities by focusing on a particular policy area, such as precollege preparedness or after-school assistance. Others described in the report are joint projects of cities and universities around infrastructure enhancements, such as Virginia Commonwealth University's longtime urban development efforts in concert with the City of Richmond, Virginia. In addition, some cases illustrate the need for universities to make their surrounding neighborhoods safer from crime and blight as a means to attract and retain both prospective students and faculty.

Many of these collaborations are entrepreneurially oriented partnerships where university real estate needs loom large.[2] Many times, these types of partnerships assist universities in locating private investment capital for their projects, such as additional outsourced residential capacity. Between 2011 and 2016, these public-private partnerships tripled to more than $3 billion.[3] In these cases, universities aim to find financial support for their campus needs while shifting some of the risk to private third parties who accept that exposure in search of short-term profits.

While there is much to recommend in a number of these types of partnerships, at least for the academic institutions and their financial backers, they are not socially and politically transformative partnerships. They primarily feature mutually beneficial financial goals for each participating entity. In contrast, I have argued throughout this book that the civic imperative for higher education revolves around partnering with local neighborhoods to assist them in gaining greater control of their own destiny to increase the menu of opportunities for their residents while simultaneously ushering in greater academic and civic learning for university students. These are transformative partnerships, shaping deep reforms within the university and the local community. In short, the transformative partnerships are about building an interracial and equitable democracy founded on a fair and dynamic economy.

We have referred to these partnerships between universities and neighborhoods as anchor partnerships. The term and the concept of anchor institutions are attractive but are vulnerable to misuse. I have encountered business collaborations that have deployed the anchor concept in urban areas but use it to describe the speculative development initiatives of a purely private corporate venture. One example is a short statement, "Kith Signs on to Anchor Williamsburg's 25 Kent," promoting a privately developed mixed-use building in Brooklyn's inner-city Williamsburg neighborhood, that I introduced earlier in this book.[4] While not intentionally deceiving the lay reader, the use of the term "anchor" in certain settings creates a more attractive and suggestive approach to what is clearly a new player in the fast-gentrifying neighborhood. For reasons such as this, I prefer using the label "university-neighborhood partnerships" because it is more declarative about who constitutes the partnership, both politically and economically. However, the existing currency for this work functions under the anchor nomenclature.

The anchor concept is the most compelling organizing principle within the world of civic engagement and higher education. It has served as an organizing principle for university-neighborhood partnerships, most notably in the work of a policy-oriented group spearheaded by Ira Harkavy at the University of Pennsylvania. It gained immediate acceptance as a vision of how universities could become more engaged in their civic missions. The "anchor" term signifies that those institutions that are highly unlikely to move from a neighborhood are therefore "moored" in place. Schools, libraries, churches, colleges, and universities are examples of institutions that are settled in place. Unlike corporations or other private arrangements that happen to be located in a particular community but are capable of moving for reasons of greater profitability or comparative advantage, anchor institutions are keyed into the fabric of a neighborhood. They are assumed to be significant local employers with fixed assets, so relocation would be prohibitive.[5]

The Anchor Institution Task Force (AITF) was formed in 2008 to advise the U.S. Department of Housing and Urban Development on how to deploy universities in solving urban challenges. Larger universities and their medical and educational institutions held a particular interest in joining the network of leaders.

David Maurrasse, the founder of consulting practice Marga Inc. and an associate research scholar at Columbia University's School of International and Public Affairs, serves as facilitator of approximately 900 individual members of AITF. The task force maintains key subgroups in economic development, health care and health disparities, K–12 schools, and higher education. Participants from across the United States and Canada, as well as a number of international institutions including but not limited to the Republic of Ireland, Northern Ireland, the Council of Europe, South Africa, and a number of Eastern and Western European nations, attend the annual meeting. The anchor model has become a compelling organizing concept for building broad coalitions with higher education institutions across urban policy areas through the collaboration of nonprofits, governmental agencies, and private interests.

This flurry of exciting engagement has led to some important demarcations for what I have termed the transformative partnerships between universities and their neighborhoods. First and foremost, the emphasis on place-based commitments is central. Equally important to AITF's definition of anchor work, the commitment to democratically organized partnerships and the focus on social equity and social justice are foundational values.

In 2012, Rita Axelroth Hodges and Steve Dubb began a helpful accounting of the new anchor partnerships with their book, *The Road Half Traveled: University Engagement at a Crossroads.*[6] Not only did they detail the anchor work of a number of leading universities, but they also provided a typology of different leadership roles they played. They categorized these differing leadership strategies as universities acting as facilitator, leader, or convener.

I will employ these strategies in my discussion of some of the successful partnership models later in this chapter. While Hodges and Dubb's book captures some of the initial anchor partnerships, it nonetheless is an important contribution to understanding comprehensive approaches to this work.

I will focus on a handful of successful university-neighborhood partnerships as examples of their scope, design, and administration. What once was a cluster of such initiatives is now a much larger theater of participating institutions. To adequately capture that in full is worthy of a full volume by itself. My goal is to introduce the reader to the workings, impacts, and challenges of the partnerships so they may be helpful guideposts for sustaining, expanding, or, more likely, founding similar affiliations. Later, in chapter 9, I will discuss some of the difficulties in sustaining and expanding these partnerships.

Rutgers University–Newark

Newark is a city too often characterized in negative terms as struggling, unmanageable, crime-ridden, and laden with a history of political corruption.[7] In fact, Newark is a city on the rise. It is rebuilding its economic base. It is a thriving arts center. But as it changes for the better, it still faces deep issues of persistent inequality, the challenges of inequitable growth and White gentrification, and intractable health disparities.

Newark is the largest city in New Jersey. In 2019, it registered a population of just under 300,000 residents, ranking it as the 73rd largest municipality in the United States.[8] Contrast that with the fact that approximately 42 percent of Newark's children live below the poverty line and the poverty rate is 33 percent, twice the national average.[9] The city's population is approximately 12 percent White, 34 percent Latino, and 54 percent African American. However, 60 percent of the jobs in Newark are held by White people. Moreover, Newark residents hold only 18 percent of those jobs. The remainder are filled by nonresidents. The Newark school system is the fourth most segregated in the United States. This is a racialized urban setting with deep inequality, both of means and opportunity.

This is the setting for a remarkably comprehensive anchor partnership that spans educational, economic, health, artistic, and governmental institutions. Central to the success of this collaboration is the principal role played by Rutgers University, Newark, led by its chancellor, Nancy Cantor. The university's role is essential and consequential for the successes of this partnership. Cantor, a courageous and resilient leader, has a clearly stated vision for the civic mission of her university: playing "an active role in reversing this cycle of urban inequality."[10]

Rutgers University–Newark works in conjunction with the city's mayor as part of an alliance of other local anchor institutions. For instance, Newark Trust for Education focuses a number of higher education institutions, the Newark Public Schools, the City of Newark, and other partners in building a comprehensive effort on expanding postsecondary education well beyond its present footprint in Newark. Ultimately, the goal is to increase some level of higher education degree completion to 25 percent of residents by 2025 from the current rate of 18 percent.

Organizing this effort is the work of the Newark City of Learning Collaborative (NCLC), which engages a host of anchor participants, including the K–12 schools, the city's universities and colleges, and government, corporate, and nonprofit institutions. The NCLC network works to promote, nurture, support, and monitor progress in increasing postsecondary education. The main coordinator of this effort at Rutgers University–Newark is the Joseph C. Cornwall Center for Metropolitan Studies. Its mission is "bringing the campus' intellectual talent and other resources to bear on the challenges of revitalizing Newark." It offers a variety of programs, forums, workshops, research projects, and other activities to support postsecondary opportunities and education throughout the public schools and within the Newark neighborhoods. In addition, it provides an array of capacity-building initiatives throughout Newark's disenfranchised neighborhoods.

The Cornwall Center coordinates its work with sixty public schools, the New Jersey Institute of Technology (a major research university), Essex Community College, Berkeley College, Pillar College, and the other anchors so that, together, they can maximize their impact on increasing enrollment, retention, success, and completion of postsecondary degrees.

The center provides tutoring and mentoring by Rutgers undergraduates who mentor local high school students. Moreover, it provides important workshops and seminars that demystify college and how to pay for it. Just as we witnessed in Port Richmond, Staten Island, poor communities can fear postsecondary education. They fear it because it is outside their experience and they fear failure in attempting to even dream of postsecondary education for their children. The Cornwall Center plays key roles in setting greater expectations for these children and providing direct educational services that allow these children to find early and steady educational success along the path to two- and four-year college degrees. Ultimately, these investments will pay dividends for these students and the Newark community, increasing the educational capacity and employability of its residents, their incomes, and that of the local economy. An accelerator effect will expand the economic prosperity of a once economically abandoned city.

Rutgers–Newark provides critical support for inner-city high school teachers. At Shabazz High School, development opportunities are provided for faculty and staff. Often overlooked, these teachers and support staff are the courageous and inventive educators who directly shape the educational lives of their students. Without additional support of every kind, partnership efforts can stall, if not falter. In addition, Rutgers–Newark engages disconnected youth who have left high school or college. The goal is to resettle them into schools with the appropriate support for their ultimate reengagement with learning and assist them in degree completion. Rutgers–Newark is part of Newark 2020: Hire, Buy, Live Local. Built across the educational partnership, the goal of this initiative is to dramatically expand the economic assets of the educational institutions and other anchors within Newark. The goal is to increase the annual monetary impact of these efforts from $2.5 million to $100 million. One of the Newark 2020 goals is to significantly increase minority-owned local business.

In the arts, Rutgers–Newark and its anchor partners are building a significant imprint. Nancy Cantor is not alone in her belief that the performing and fine arts, along with design and media, are definite foundational pieces that not only serve the civic spirit of the city but also promote the authentic and long-ignored voices of the community. As we witnessed in Port Richmond on a smaller scale with its Voices of Port Richmond, the arts create a remarkable sense of agency. As such, they have a major impact on civic mindedness and community self-confidence.

The arts and design are engines of personal, social, and economic progress. Rutgers–Newark was an essential part of the repurposing and redevelopment of the historic Hahne and Company building downtown. A legendary Newark department store that had atrophied in the city's economic decline, it now serves as a major multipurpose retail and arts center, the latter run by the university. This is a beacon for the arts in Newark, with participants from all ages. The anchors included the city, local developers, and national investors. The Rutgers participation was essential for the center's realization. The building is a dramatic symbol of the old and revitalized Newark coming together and taking back some of its past, while forging a robust future.

Rutgers University–Newark is the most advanced anchor partnership model in the United States. Its breadth is remarkable, ranging across the main areas of need in the city. It has more dimensions than I have mentioned here, including those addressing health inequalities, prison education, and criminal justice reform. Its success depends on smart, resilient, and courageous leadership that starts with the chancellor and her excellent senior team and carries through large numbers of other key staff and faculty members. It is embedded into the fabric of the university. Just as President Judith

Ramaley helped Portland State rediscover its institutional and civic mission, Chancellor Cantor guided Rutgers–Newark to revitalize itself as it partnered with the city's renaissance. Rutgers–Newark exemplifies the central argument of this book, namely, that poor neighborhoods and universities, both large and small, can be allies and anchors for one another. Together they can rise and flourish.

The University of Pennsylvania and West Philadelphia Schools

The University of Pennsylvania (UPenn) and its Netter Center for Community Partnerships are the epicenter for the anchor institutions movement. The center's director, Ira Harkavy, is the national leader for anchors. All who have worked with him revere him as a national treasure. How UPenn and Netter rose to this national level is an interesting story. The scope of the university's work and the breadth of its influence are quite extensive. The institution is the national and global mentor for anchor partnerships.

UPenn is an admired Ivy League institution with a world-renowned reputation for its advanced research in almost every academic discipline. In addition, it is a cutting-edge medical and scientific research center. The Nobel Prize has been awarded to twenty-eight laureates from the university. In the past ten years, the university's scholars received six Nobel Prizes. Founded by Benjamin Franklin in 1749, by every measure, UPenn is at the pinnacle of higher education.

In contrast, the City of Philadelphia is suffering from deep pockets of racialized inequality. Despite its economic vitality as the producer of the ninth largest gross domestic product among American cities, Philadelphia is held back by its inability to significantly increase the menu of opportunities available to its poor neighborhoods. One in four families are below the federal poverty line. In fact, Philadelphia's poverty rate of 25.7 percent contrasts with the national poverty rate of 13.4 percent. Median family income has declined in the past four years. By national standards, more than 30 percent of the city's children live in poverty, but if measured by self-sufficiency benchmarks, close to 43 percent of its families fall below the poverty line.[11]

Among the big cities in the United States, Philadelphia is the fourth most segregated, trailing only Chicago, Milwaukee, and Atlanta. It is home to 1.6 million residents divided demographically as 44 percent Black, 36 percent White, 13.6 percent Latino, and 7 percent Asian. In a city known for its large cluster of colleges and universities, only 29 percent of Philadelphia's residents earned bachelor's degrees or higher. This is disappointing but almost inevitable given the unequal distribution of income, wealth, and opportunity.

In the mid-1990s, these contradictions collided. For decades, the neighborhood surrounding the fast-expanding footprint around the prestigious university was in economic decline and escalating in street crime. Tragically, in 1996, a researcher at UPenn was fatally stabbed when leaving work. The crescendo of fear, anger, and disappointment engulfed President Judith Rodin and Mayor Ed Rendell.[12] Determined to seriously increase the university's previous efforts to address the urban pathologies in the West Philadelphia area near the campus, President Rodin introduced the West Philadelphia Initiative (WPI).

In 1998, for example, the university partnered with the School District of Philadelphia and the Philadelphia Federation of Teachers to launch a new and comprehensive K–8 school in West Philadelphia specifically to provide a model school for this underserved community. Named after a legendary University of Pennsylvania African American alumna, Sadie Tanner Mossell Alexander, the school officially accepted first graders in 2001 and then phased in all grades in 2004.[13] The school is assisted by UPenn's Graduate School of Education as well as many UPenn undergraduates. Both provide a rich array of educational opportunities in science, reading, mathematics, and technology, achieving a rich educational foundation for students in West Philadelphia.

Although some university civic work had begun around 1985, President Sheldon Hackney in 1992 approved the creation of what became known as the Netter Center for Community Partnerships.[14] It institutionalized and elevated the civic mission within the complex organizational structure of competing schools and programs, all rich with prestigious and accomplished scholars. President Hackney made this commitment a major priority, and his genius was in appointing Ira Harkavy to lead it. Hackney, as noted, was followed by Judith Rodin, who increased UPenn's commitment. After ten years, Amy Gutmann, an accomplished political theorist, followed Rodin as the next president. She doubled down on this work.

Harkavy had spent many years at the university as an undergraduate and later a successful graduate student in history. He knew the West Philadelphia area, and he had positive relationships in the community. Most important, he was determined to have UPenn serve as a leader in addressing the racial and class inequalities in the neighborhood. He understood the university's self interest in creating a safer climate for students, staff, and faculty members. He was not about establishing a public relations effort to front the continued real estate ambitions of the university. He had the vision and determination to build a true reciprocal partnership where both parties benefited. He also knew that for this to work to be successful, it would require the Netter Center to serve as the internal organ for galvanizing the research, service learning, and outreach assets of UPenn. He knew intuitively that the center must be under the academic wing of the administration. It started within the

School of Arts and Sciences and in 1992 it became a university-wide center housed in the president's office as well as Arts and Sciences. This created academic legitimacy and access to those educational assets.

Harkavy established some basic guidelines for the scope of UPenn's role in West Philadelphia to ensure that it would have a genuine impact on community prosperity, and the Netter Center operated accordingly. It moved the university away from the role as a real estate entrepreneur to one of community ally.

Today, the Netter Center holds a broad menu of programs that continues to deepen and expand in Philadelphia and to build the center's role as a national and global leader. At its core lies the University Assisted Community Schools Initiative, which involves a number of programs and interacts with many of the academic pieces of the university. The center sponsors and coordinates hundreds of community-based learning courses across the many schools and academic programs. The programs mainly support the community schools in West Philadelphia by providing an army of UPenn students to support K–12 students, their teachers, and staff during the school day and in after-school programs. This work links the Academically Based Community Service (ABCS) courses with tutoring, mentoring, and college guidance in the schools.[15] In addition, the ABCS courses "focus on action-oriented community problem solving and the integration of research, teaching, learning, and service as well as reflection on the service experience."[16] Subjects range from poverty, race, and crime to nutrition, environment, and many others. They link the university's brilliant scholars and their students with K–12 students in engaging the immediate realities in West Philadelphia.

At one of the neighborhood's middle schools, Netter's Civic Youth Action Partnership involves undergraduates working with preadolescents in holding policy debates, introducing them to concepts of classical and modern political theories, and running their middle-school student government meetings. Another Netter program, Moelis Access Science, provides key support to stimulate and develop STEM subjects for K–12 grades. The Penn Reading Initiative is a one-on-one tutoring program to enhance reading skills of second- and third-grade students in West Philadelphia. The center oversees the Agatston Urban Nutrition Initiative, which promotes nutrition education, food access, and physical fitness for elementary school students in Southwest and West Philadelphia. The program has reached more than six thousand students and their families. In conjunction with the Perelman School of Medicine and UPenn's School of Veterinary Medicine, the Center also runs a high school mentoring program for underrepresented high school students. Finally, a number of other Netter Center programs work on environmental challenges, financial literacy and education, new ventures, and more. In short, the Netter

Center is responsible for a comprehensive educational footprint in West Philadelphia.

The university's commitments do not end here. UPenn redirected its hiring, purchasing, and investment portfolios to support the local economy. This has a multi-million-dollar impact. In addition, the university has a program that subsidizes home purchasing for eligible employees in West Philadelphia. It established a housing upgrade for over two hundred apartments and made them available to local moderate-income renters and buyers. In addition, the university made significant improvements to street safety and upgraded the neighborhood through new investment in retail outlets. Overall, the university spent $122 million in 2015 in West Philadelphia and its health system hired more than 1,500 local residents.

I have not touched on all aspects of UPenn's community imprint, but what I have presented should provide the reader with an understanding of its anchor vision and practice. What is truly remarkable is that with all the intense pressures on one of the world's leading research universities to maintain and fund cutting edge research in all of its academic programs and schools and all that goes with it, UPenn is a bold example of those standards and ambitions not limiting its equally impressive and well-earned reputation as a model of civic and democratic responsibility.

The role of institutional leadership is critical and indelible. Ira Harkavy, his remarkable, brilliant, and resilient staff, and the pointed commitments of President Hackney, and later Presidents Rodin and Gutmann all proved to be decisive in forging this civic pathway for the university. This raises the question for all of the models that I will introduce, including my own dear Wagner College: Will these deep commitments hold over time if the next generation of civic leaders and university presidents falls short of the standards set by these founders, visionaries, and practitioners? I will take up this topic at the end of this chapter and later in this book.

Augsburg University and the Cedar-Riverside Partnership

On May 25, 2020, George Floyd was murdered in Minneapolis by a White police officer who knelt on his throat for eight minutes and thirty-eight seconds while three other officers looked on without interfering. A sizable crowd was imploring the White officer to stop kneeling on Floyd, who was helpless, unarmed, and begging for his life. "I can't breathe," he kept saying. This is sadly similar to Eric Garner's plea to police officers in Staten Island's St. George neighborhood, down the boulevard from my Wagner College campus. In Floyd's case, he supposedly handed a retail store clerk a counterfeit $20 bill. In Eric Garner's case, he was illegally selling individual cigarettes on a street corner. Two Black men, without resisting arrest, were killed for no justifiable reason and both were pleading, "I can't breathe."

These are two examples of systemic racism and personal bigotry. The history of the United States is littered with examples of racial brutality.[17] They initiate with the origins of slavery in 1619 and they continue today in what has been characterized as the new Jim Crow. This reality is dramatically illustrated in the statistics on the school-prison pipeline that I cited in chapter 1 and in the stories like the death of Freddie Gray in Baltimore. Anchor partnerships are not the answer to this reality, but they can begin to fortify neighborhoods by opening doors to the forgotten, frightened, and subjugated citizens who are trapped in shadow communities. The Port Richmond and West Philadelphia communities are prime examples.

Longfellow is a mixed neighborhood of approximately 5,000 residents, and 60 percent of them are White. Minneapolis is a city with a population of 416,000 with roughly the same demographics. The city encompasses a number of diverse neighborhoods. The Cedar-Riverside neighborhood, which sits not too far from Longfellow, is a highly diverse community that is the home of what we can call the Somali diaspora. During and after the Somali Civil War in the late 1980s, many people fled for their safety. One would think refugees from a hot climate would seek a similar environment for their safety, but 74,000 of them found an ally in the Lutheran refugee resettlement efforts in the Minneapolis-St. Paul Twin Cities.

As with any displaced group, the Somali population's adjustment and acceptance into a geographically and culturally different location proved to be overwhelming. Redeploying from a mostly rural, poor setting to a modern, postindustrial city was a recipe for disorientation and isolation. Alone and unprepared to succeed in this new advanced urban milieu, the new immigrants struggled without meaningful jobs. Unemployment is approximately 18 percent in their neighborhood, compared with 3 percent for the entire state of Minnesota. Many finally settled in the Cedar-Riverside neighborhood, which happened to be close to a small private Lutheran college, now renamed Augsburg University. The president is Paul Pribbenow, PhD, another remarkable leader. When he took office, he authored a more inclusive and democratic vision of the university's civic mission.

With the arrival and settlement of the Somali refugees and their formation of a diaspora in Minneapolis, Augsburg faced an inflection point as a faith-based institution of higher education. As poverty grew, along with its ensuing coefficients of economic vulnerability and racial separation, how would Augsburg react? Would it see itself as an unwitting victim of a declining neighborhood or would it redouble its civic and spiritual mission as a shepherd for its new neighbors and partner with them in building a community rich with dignity, safety, and opportunity? Against this backdrop, President Pribbenow formulated Augsburg's renewed vision, which he termed an "urban settlement."

Drawn from his own scholarship on Hull House, Jane Addams's legendary settlement for the poor in Chicago, Pribbenow instantly grasped Augsburg's anchor responsibility within its own community. He was committed to a place-based strategy for both learning and living in search of the good community. He realized that the assets of the university could be deployed to create a positive impact on the community, to increase student learning, and to help the university overall. While Augsburg had a long history of service, it would now step forward as a local and national leader in university-neighborhood partnerships. It is now a model of civic purpose and higher learning, especially for smaller private institutions.

To this end, Augsburg helped found the Cedar-Riverside Partnership encompassing the downtown Minneapolis Somali community and an emerging Mexican one as well. While this is the epicenter of Augsburg's civic involvement at Augsburg, it does not account for all of its civic work. In addition to international outreach in Mexico, Nigeria, and Namibia, the core campus is home to the Sabo Center housing the university's place-based work. Undergraduates have a vast amount of community-based learning courses around the many civic commitments, as well as many volunteer opportunities.

The essence of the anchor work revolves around the Cedar-Riverside Partnership (CRP), which was created to assist the neighborhood in rising above its economic and social circumstances. CRP is composed of approximately thirteen nonprofit and governmental institutional partners, including both the City of Minneapolis and Hennepin County. Augsburg University plays a leadership role. The partners have focused on transit issues, economic development, youth opportunities, education, health disparities, and public safety. In 2017, the partnership launched the Cedar-Riverside Opportunity Center in the middle of the neighborhood. It holds job fairs, job training programs, counseling for at-risk students, safety and crime education, early childhood programs, health and academic education initiatives for grades K–5, services for disabled youth, homework help workshops in conjunction with the local library, STEM development training, and job opportunities.

The job fairs and training programs have been very successful. In the 2019 Cedar-Riverside Partnership Annual Report, 862 individuals participated and 470 acquired jobs.[18] Their job retention rate was 79 percent. The multi-institutional partnership has brought light and hope to this neighborhood. You will find a resilient army of Augsburg students and faculty engaged in any number of these programs through their community-based learning courses and direct work with the Sabo Center. Faculty are involved in community-based research on the challenges confronted in the neighborhood and in the city. In the East African Student to Teacher (EAST) Program, Augsburg is preparing East African teachers for the Minneapolis School System while they are working with young Mexican Dreamers on their educational advancement.

All of this engagement has reconfigured the diversity on the Augsburg campus. The entering class in 2017 was 53 percent students of color. This is a remarkable change over the past twenty years. The entire image of the place has been transformed as Augsburg has become a part of the Cedar-Riverside community.

One personal story illustrates this rather vividly. A few years ago, I was visiting the Augsburg campus as part of a large group of college representatives and Campus Compact staff who were attending a national meeting that was charting a new direction for Compact. Over three days, we toured a number of the civic engagement sites, which were quite impressive. We held all of the conference sessions in the university's very modern chapel/community center. Noticeably propped in front of the many worktables we assembled for our small conversations was a podium-like altar. Just to the left was a large, maybe eight-foot, portrait of a Christ-like African figure. After two days of long meetings in this room, I pulled Paul Pribbenow aside and naively asked, "Who is that?" He calmly turned to me and said, "That is our African Jesus." He went on to say how the entire school was undergoing change in light of the considerable diversification of the student body. I then asked what happened to the standard portrait of Jesus. Seemingly waiting for this delicious moment of personal and institutional pride, Pribbenow said, "Oh, you mean the Norwegian Jesus? Look behind you, way up there in the balcony seats. He hangs on the back wall." Sometimes a picture does convey a thousand words.

The Augsburg model demonstrates that college and university partnerships need not be exclusive to wealthy institutions or publicly funded ones. It is affordable and, more impressively, it is a galvanizing mission for a deep and meaningful education and preparation for civic leadership in an inclusive democracy. In Paul Pribbenow's own words,

> an authentic engagement with immigrants means that colleges and universities must expand their understanding of academic mission. Our traditional values about excellence and rigor; our organizational structures related to power sharing; and our sense of how teaching and learning occur—all of these are challenged by the immigrant experience. We meet immigrants in our neighborhood who teach our students and all of us important lessons about life in the world.[19]

Rutgers University–Camden

Today, Camden, New Jersey, has a population of approximately 77,000. In 1950, 124,000 resided in the city and 86 percent were White. Today, the city is more than 80 percent African American and Latino. Economically, it is a victim of the job loss in manufacturing as a result of Vietnam-era deindustrialization. While a modest economic recovery is underway, the vast majority of jobs are in health care and education. Unemployment hovers around 20 percent, more than double the rate for the state of New Jersey.[20] Approximately 40 percent of its residents and 54 percent of its children live below the federal poverty line. Additionally, of those over the age of twenty-five, 63 percent do not hold a high school diploma and only 10 percent have earned a two- or four-year college degree.

In 2013, then Governor Chris Christie removed the authority of the public school system as a result of the high school graduation rate falling to 49 percent. Of the Camden public high school students taking the SATs only 2 percent scored 1550 or above. The national average is 43 percent. Only 19 percent of third graders were reading at a proficient level and 30 percent of eighth graders were proficient in reading and math. In 2014, 23 of the 26 schools in the city districts had the lowest schoolwide proficiency in the entire state of New Jersey.[21] These were not new markers but rather part of a continuing downward trend.

In response to this educational and economic tragedy, Rutgers University–Camden framed an anchor institution-inspired strategic response.[22] This was a change for the university. For most of the years since its founding in the 1920s, the university focused its gaze inward. With the leadership of two consecutive visionary and practical-minded chancellors, namely, Wendell Pritchett and Phoebe Hadden, the university took on the challenges of the city and its failing schools. Aided by smart and resilient staff, Rutgers University–Camden initiated and built a collage of civic partnerships and initiatives to address the lack of college awareness, readiness, and success.

The Rutgers–Camden strategic approach is to create an educational pipeline, similar to the Wagner College-PRP educational pipeline. Toward this end, the campus leadership augmented a sizable number of course offerings with community-based learning opportunities. Aimed at addressing the challenges within Camden, these academically based civic experiences are popular. Currently, 75 percent of the university's undergraduates take these courses. They account for 436,000 hours of direct engagement spread across 216 academic courses, which span the breadth of academic disciplines.

These and other forms of civic engagement play out in a number of different arenas. Along with the Camden City School System, the Mastery Charter Schools, and the Camden County Charter Schools, the university founded the Rutgers North Camden Partnership. This collaboration involves pre-K through grade twelve students, parents, families, and community members. The partnership is focused on preparing and sustaining college awareness and success from the very earliest grades through high school to college admission. The partnership works on both academic and social emotional growth of students. It enrolls approximately 300 students. Additionally, the partnership continues its work by supporting college success and completion.

The Ignite Program assists grades four through eight in STEM subjects, particularly in wellness and health issues. The goal of this initiative is to demystify college for first-generation students and low-income youngsters and help them envision college attendance and completion as an expectation. As these young students are drawn onto campus, their familiarity grows and their personal apprehensions decline. What may have been strange and feared now becomes comfortable and intimate. I personally witnessed this over and over again at Wagner College with our Port Richmond students.

The Rutgers Future Scholars program takes fifty promising first-generation, low-income students from the Camden Schools to the campus during the summer. The students are rising eighth graders who enroll in a campus academic program. They continue in academic enrichment and mentoring programs year-round throughout high school. The Hill Family Center for College Access works with low-income and first-generation college students in grades eleven and twelve by holding workshops on campus and in the schools around issues of higher education options, financial aid, and admissions processes. These can seem to be insurmountable challenges for families and students foreign to college attendance. They alone can reignite fears of failure and create psychological barriers that prevent the pursuit of the admissions process.

The university partnered with the LEAP Academy in founding the LEAP Academy University School, one of thirteen inaugural public charter schools in Camden. It covers pre-K through grade twelve with a successful high school and college placement program that holds a 100 percent success rate. The partnership serves more than fifteen hundred students throughout the K–12 grades. Finally, Rutgers University–Camden initiated a "bridging the gap" program addressing issues of financial support and college affordability at Rutgers.

Other aspects of the university's civic work in Camden involve nursing and other related fields that address the city's needs. In the end, the Rutgers

University–Camden campus has reinvented itself as an engaged learning institution that is a steward of place along with its neighbors. It is committed to educating its mostly first-generation and highly diverse student body as agents of change and civic professionals while helping to elevate a city facing a long period of decline. In the process, these students and their faculty mentors are bringing along new generations of leaders who are learning the arts of democracy early in life as they fortify their community and elevate the lives of their neighbors. Along the way, the Rutgers University–Camden campus has never been as intellectually alive, civically engaged, and nationally recognized.

Miami Dade College and Miami's Neighborhoods of Overton and Liberty City

There are two popular images of Miami, Florida. One features economic growth, opulence, and leisure. The other depicts racialized poverty, illegal drugs, and criminal gangs. The two Miamis are a genuine tale of two cities. Overton and Liberty City are two neighborhoods that are linked to the "poor" Miami. Demographically, they are both heavily African American.

Both neighborhoods share a linked and somewhat racist past.[23] Overton was formed as part of the incorporation of the City of Miami in 1896. Given the enforcement of Jim Crow laws and its rigid codes, Black Americans were restricted from living in "White" Miami or Miami Beach. They even needed passes to enter Coral Gables or Miami Beach. They were confined to "Colored Town," which was the original name of the Overton neighborhood. It filled up with both middle- and working-class African Americans and grew steadily in population, as well as neglect, through to the Great Depression. In 1933, President Franklin Roosevelt ushered in the development of a new section of Miami that was called Liberty Square. It was a novel Southern housing initiative. Overton was suffering from deteriorating housing, and Liberty Square was designed to alleviate the decline. Over the next twenty years, it was a thriving community for middle-income Black Americans. Eventually, it became known as Liberty City. After the construction of U.S. Interstate 95 through Overton, many of its poor flooded into Liberty City and its African American middle class moved out.

Today, Overton's population is approximately 7,000 residents, composed of 75 percent Black Americans and 20 percent Latino. The neighborhood has a median household income of $30,707 annually. In Liberty City, the median family household income is approximately $21,418.[24] Near these Black neighborhoods sits Little Havana, a community of approximately 50,000. Its population is 85 percent Latino Americans, largely Cuban, and

15 percent Nicaraguans and Hondurans. Little Havana has a poverty rate of 37 percent and a median household income of $21,618. The level of income inequality gap in Miami is the second largest in the United States among the major metropolitan areas. Approximately 14 percent of Miami residents live at or below the federal poverty line, but the Overton rate is 39 percent, Liberty City's is 42 percent, and Little Havana's is 37 percent. Yet surrounding this grim reality, Miami is home to thirty billionaires, and the state is one of the top five American communities for millennial millionaires. The level of inequality is deep and wide in Miami, and without meaningful intervention, it promises to worsen.

In 1959, Miami Dade Community College was founded in the midst of these dynamics. At its outset, it was a segregated institution in compliance with the South's Jim Crow laws, but it soon desegregated. Eventually it was approved to offer four-year degrees, becoming known as simply Miami Dade College (MDC). Today, it has eight campuses, one of which is a medical center, and twenty-one outreach centers throughout the county. With 165,000 students and 6,500 on staff, it is the largest higher education institution in the Florida system and the second largest college or university in the United States.

From 1995 until 2019, it was led by an outstanding president and transformative leader, Eduardo Padrón. He provided a remarkable civic vision for this expanding institution. Confronted by the growing metrics of inequality, Padrón understood that to improve life in this city, economic opportunity must expand dramatically. Increasing education, particularly higher education, must be made easily available to a large number of those left behind economically and socially. While the college always was viewed as an engine for increasing employability, Padrón firmly placed MDC as an anchor institution within the entire city and county.

As a Cuban refugee himself, Padrón understood the difficulty for immigrants in attaining English language fluency while trying to restart their lives within a world of urban inequality. As a former student of MDC and a distinguished economist with a PhD from the University of Florida, he returned to MDC as a faculty member. When he assumed the presidency, his gaze was on creating vibrant pathways for educational attainment at every level within Dade County. His goal was to make MDC an engine of social change for these communities. The scope of MDC's imprint on civic and economic life is vast. It focuses on increasing economic opportunity, career and job readiness, and civic prosperity. I will offer a few key illustrations from the vast portfolio of the college's work.

MDC offers more than 5,900 service-learning courses that are aligned respectively with 220 community partners. To ensure depth of learning and quality contribution to the community partners, MDC follows strict protocols on the nature and depth of field and service experiences—and reflection upon them. Simply organizing, administering, and assessing these many engagements require major resources and staffing. To accomplish this is stunning, particularly when we consider that MDC is a commuter school of predominantly first-generation college students of many different ages with varying family obligations.

Most students must work while attending MDC. For example, all nursing and dental studies students are required to take these service courses for hundreds of hours as part of their major concentrations. Many of them need to work in order to afford the cost of attendance while contributing to their family's budgets. These circumstances could serve as barriers to placing service and field-based engagement into what are demanding personal schedules.

This major educational and civic institutional priority is managed by the Institute for Civic Engagement and Democracy (CED), which also administers approximately 300 formal partnerships with local community agencies. These span a vast array of disciplines such as animal and veterinary care, adult education, literacy, public schools, child services, tutoring programs, criminal justice and at-risk youth, community improvement, culture and the arts, services for the elderly, environmental and scientific initiatives, HIV/AIDS, health care, developmental disabilities, homelessness, hunger, and substance abuse.

MDC also operates a large America Reads program through the CED as well as a free GED program on six of its eight campuses for those who dropped out of high school and are seeking to complete their degree. MDC operates the Carrie Meek Entrepreneurial Education Center in support of increasing small business in the Black business corridor. The center also works with high school students interested in entrepreneurship through credit bearing opportunities. Other examples of partnership work include a Hospitality Institute that offers job training and the School of Community Education, which offers a series of similar outreach programs in the Overton neighborhood. MDC's Medical Center partnered with the Miami Rescue Mission through the Nursing Program, with its faculty and students performing health screenings.

These are a few examples of the MDC partnership model, and in particular, with its shadow neighborhoods of Overton and Liberty City. The sheer scope of the MDC civic footprint is impressive as well as strategic. This is an anchor institution that partners with other higher education institutions as well as health care, criminal justice, and the school system throughout Miami Dade County. It has and is bringing higher education to those often left out and largely ignored in our society. In doing so, it has inspired a city and its neighborhoods to reach beyond their circumstances. Through its dedicated civic work, it offers them a chance to create personal agency in a world that seemingly only offers them predestined lives of low-paying service jobs, substandard housing, and lower quality health care. They are expected to accept those silently. MDC exists and works to reverse that inevitability. MDC has become a national leader in modeling a renewed civic mission for higher education. In 2016, then President Barack Obama awarded President Padrón the Medal of Freedom for his determined and dignified leadership and MDC's accomplishments.

University of Nebraska Omaha and The Weitz Center

Before I leave this chapter on different types of universities and anchor partnerships, it is important to provide an example of an innovative arrangement between a major university and its nonprofit community partners. Under the leadership of then Chancellor John Christensen, the University of Nebraska Omaha developed a large civic commitment to the City of Omaha. It provided an extensive service-learning curriculum and numerous other engagements. It expanded into sustained partnerships with a range of non-profits in addressing genuine city needs in the public schools and challenged neighborhoods.

Christensen embarked on a unique approach to sustaining the university's civic work, particularly the partnerships. He developed the concept of resident partners on the campus. Securing a generous private gift of $24 million in 2014, the university built a new 70,000 square-foot building to house up to thirty-seven of its nonprofit partners in what is now called the Barbara Weitz Community Engagement Center. The partner organizations range across the spectrum of community, including health, environmental, youth services, education, and civic entities. They hold meetings and offer forums, dialogues, trainings, speakers, conferences, cultural events, and community meetings.

The center saves these institutional partners more than $9 million in rent and fees, thus allowing them critical support and resources that help to ensure their fiscal viability. The University of Nebraska Omaha houses its well-regarded Service Learning Academy in the Weitz Center. The shared community space among the university's two hundred undergraduate and graduate service-learning courses and their administration allows for an unusual intimacy and reciprocity between the campus's civic engagement programs and its community partners. I refer to this model as the residential anchor approach. It is a very interesting model that is appropriate in certain settings. Although it may be less efficacious for other universities, it works handsomely for Omaha. The university invites Omaha to share quarters and create a larger sense of a shared neighborhood.

Summary

There are literally hundreds of examples of full or partial university anchor partnerships with their surrounding neighborhoods. I have chosen seven at different types of colleges and universities. I presented Wagner College in the previous chapter and six others in this one. My goal was to expose the reader to the rich variety of institutions, private and public, large and small, research, comprehensive, liberal arts, and community college, as examples. Neither size nor academic mission precludes these partnerships.

I could have chosen other examples, but these are the ones I know best. Others to explore are the University of Louisville, James Madison University, Johns Hopkins University, Drexel University, DeAnza Community College, Morehouse College, Spelman College, and Duquesne University. I am quite confident that many others are equally compelling models of anchor work. For a more thorough accounting, I would suggest that the reader consult the websites of Campus Compact, the Coalition of Urban and Metropolitan Universities (CUMU), the Association of State Colleges and Universities (ASCU), the Anchor Institutions Task Force, and the Civic Learning and Democratic Engagement (CLDE) website.

The key point that I insist upon is that the futures of colleges and universities and those of shadow communities are intertwined and codependent. The examples I have presented offer illustrations, not blueprints, for these relationships. Every neighborhood, along with each university or college, has distinct legacies, locations, and people. Each finds its own pathway for building these partnerships. In the next chapter I will present some of the students, faculty, partners, and national leaders in their own voices so the reader can feel the impact, success, failures, and challenges involved in this work.

Notes

1. See "The Campus as City: Crucial Strategies to Bolster Town-Gown Relations and Run 21st-Century Institutions," *Chronicle of Higher Education*, Washington DC, 2019.

2. For a review of the entrepreneurial anchor, see Gavin Luter and Henry Louis Taylor, "Anchor Institutions and Urban Society: A Review of the Literature," Center for Urban Studies, University of Buffalo, 2012; Burton R. Clark, *Creating*

Entrepreneurial Universities: Organizational Pathways of Transformation (New York: Pergamon Press, 1998).

3. "The Campus as City," 12.

4. See "Kith Signs onto Anchor Williamsburg 25 Kent" in www.businesswire .com/news/home/20191217.

5. See "The Anchor Institution Tool Kit," The Netter Center, University of Pennsylvania. See also Luter and Taylor, "Anchor Institutions and Urban Society."

6. Rita A. Hodges and Steve Dubb, *The Road Half Travelled: University Engagement at a Crossroads* (East Lansing, MI: Michigan State University Press, 2012).

7. See Jessica Mazzola, "We Asked What People Thought of Newark, Their Answers may Surprise You," New Jersey Advance Media for NJ.com, July 16, 2017.

8. See U.S. Census Bureau, U.S. Government, Washington DC, 2020.

9. Nancy Cantor, Tai Cooper, Marcia Brown, and Peter Englot, "Tackling 'the Two Americas' with City-Wide Collaboration in Newark," *Journal of Anchor Institutions and Communities* 2 (2019).

10. Cantor et al., "Tackling 'the Two Americas' with City-Wide Collaboration in Newark."

11. Nancy Cantor, "Anchor Institution Coalitions to Reduce Urban Inequality" (keynote address at the launch of the New Jersey Coalition of Anchor Institutions, May 2017).

12. For these statistics, see U.S. Census Bureau for Philadelphia. See also Alfred Lubrano, "Around the Country, Incomes Are Rising. In Philly, They're Falling," *Philadelphia Inquirer*, Sept. 13, 2018; *Philadelphia Magazine*, September 22, 2015; Farrah Parks and Marianne Bellesorte, "Philadelphia's Poverty Problem Is Bigger than Ever Imagined," https://generosity.org, March 16, 2020.

13. See Ira Harkavy, Mathew Hartley, Rita Axelroth Hodges, and Joann Weeks, "The Promise of University-Assisted Community Schools to Transform American Schooling: A Report from the Field, 1985–2012," *Peabody Journal of Education* 88 (2013): 525–540.

14. See Harley Etienne, *Pushing Back the Gates: Neighborhood Perspectives on University Driven Revitalization in West Philadelphia* (Philadelphia: Temple University Press, 2012).

15. Etienne, *Pushing Back the Gates*, chapter 2.

16. Harkavy et al., "The Promise of University-Assisted Community Schools," 530.

17. See https://pennalexander.philasd.org.

18. There is a rich history regarding the use of brutal force to enforce the American system of slavery and its successor, the Jim Crow system of so-called "separate but equal." For recent scholarship, see Andrew Delbanco, *The War Before the War: Fugitive Slaves and the Struggle for America's Soul from the Revolution to the Civil War* (New York: Penguin Press, 2018); Isabel Wilkerson, *The Warmth of Other Suns: The Epic Story of America's Great Migration* (New York: Random House, 2010); Michelle Alexander, *The New Jim Crow: Mass Incarceration in the Age of Color Blindness* (New York: The New Press, 2010).

19. See *2019 Cedar Riverside Partnership Annual Report*, www.cedarriverside-partnership.org.

20. Paul Pribbenow, "Hospitality Is Not Enough: Reflections on Universities and the Immigrant Experience," *Higher Education for Diversity, Social Inclusion, and Community*, Council of Europe Higher Education Series 22 (August 2018): 143.

21. See Camden, NJ, in Wikipedia.

22. See Phoebe Haddon and Nyeema Watson, "Serving a City Invincible with Access and Engagement," *Journal of Higher Education Outreach and Engagement* 19, no. 4 (December 2015): 7. See also Phoebe Haddon and Nyeema Watson, "Opportunity and Access: Democratizing Higher Education," *Journal of Anchor Institutions and Communities* 2 (August 2019).

23. Haddon and Watson, "Serving a City Invincible" and "Opportunity and Access."

24. See Wikipedia for Overton, FL, which captures U.S. Census data and history.

7

PROFILES IN PRACTICE

Throughout this book, I have made the case for the educational, economic, and civic benefits of university anchor partnerships. Moreover, the stories have illustrated the deep educational, health, and economic inequalities in America's shadow communities. The self-interest of universities has been demonstrated. This book captures higher education's historic civic mission and the current practice of engaged universities. I have presented exemplary institutional anchor models. And while I have provided specific examples of engaged students, community partners, faculty members, and institutional leaders, it would be helpful for the reader to be exposed to a deeper illustration of the impact of this work on high school and college students, university faculty, college administrators, and community partners. This chapter is aptly titled "Profiles in Practice." It brings us to a more intimate portrait of the anchor work through the eyes of individual practitioners.[1]

In this chapter, I describe how the civic work has shaped the individuals as people. What difference has it made in their lives? How have they affected others through the anchor practice? Did they have allies, mentors, friends, family, or community members who brought them to a new or different understanding of themselves and the worlds around them? You will meet these remarkable individuals who offer a visual composite of the human face of the civic work.

Pedro Santiago, Student

On a spring afternoon on Staten Island in 2017, seventeen-year-old Pedro Santiago arrived home from PRHS. His mother was waiting patiently for him. It was a day they both had been praying about for three years. He would learn by letter whether he would be awarded a full four-year tuition, room, and board scholarship to Wagner College. So much was riding on this one letter. Pedro knew the outcome, but he wanted his mother to discover the decision on her own.

He handed her the letter saying, "Look, the letter is so thin," as if preparing her for yet another barrier to overcome in her difficult life. A single mother since she gave birth to Pedro when she was sixteen years old and living in a challenging Puerto Rican neighborhood in the Bronx, she knew all too well about social and economic barriers. At this point in her tough life, she would soon learn that she would be struggling with breast cancer in the fight of her life.

Sitting in a soft club chair, she took the letter and carefully read it. She stared at it for a long time, frozen in the moment, and finally she said out loud, "You got it, you got it." She stood up, dazed by what seemed unimaginable, threw her arms around her son, and collapsed in tears. They both were hugging and crying as they grasped the meaning of this life-changing event. Pedro Santiago would attend Wagner College for free. Four years later, he received his bachelor's degree in May 2021, finishing with a major in English and minors in sociology, civic engagement, and African American studies.

Pedro completed the three-year college preparatory program at Wagner College, the Port Richmond Partnership Leadership Academy, or what the students themselves renamed PRPLA. How he came to enroll in that program is an inspiring story because of the resiliency he and his mother showed in the face of impossible obstacles that easily defeated so many families born and raised in similar circumstances. Pedro's journey is representative of so many others fortunate in finding university and college allies who partnered with their neighborhoods.

Being born to teenage parents in a difficult locale like the Bronx usually forecasts a life more likely to lead to many dead ends. As I presented in chapter 1, reading readiness by fourth grade is a reliable predictor of high school graduation. It also is a correlation for the likelihood of eventual prison incarceration for Black and Brown boys. By the time Pedro was entering third grade, he already had been to six elementary schools. While just a young boy himself, his dad had been convicted of manslaughter when Pedro was two years old. His teenage mom raised him as best she could. They were in and out of shelters, constantly moving, trying to survive.

When his father returned to the family, Pedro was eleven years old. Life became even more challenging, with much conflict in the household. Pedro had an ideal of his father that he did not find in his daily life. He and his mom eventually moved to Staten Island and settled in the Port Richmond community, which was becoming heavily populated with Latino families, especially immigrants from Oaxaca, Mexico. Like his mom, these were hardworking people, committed to their children's welfare but saddled with limited employment skills and even more reduced opportunities. By the accident of place and time, Pedro and his mom were presented with a new opportunity. Wagner College and the leading antipoverty organization on Staten Island, Project Hospitality, had proposed to New York State that a public charter be given for a middle school aimed at, but not exclusively limited to, immigrant children in Port Richmond. Under the guidance of a most remarkable agent for social justice, Reverend Terry Troia, New World Prep was launched with a special focus on learning, leadership, and civic responsibility.

Pedro's life was in turmoil. But as chance would have it, he entered New World Prep as a seventh grader. It became his sanctuary for stability and coherence. One of his teachers at the time, Amanda Cortese, described him as a charming boy, always willing to help out with school chores. He would be the first one at school and stay all day until he was required to leave. He seemed so mature and caring. He was a little self-conscious, but he was eager to be of use. Eventually he joined the middle school leadership program, and he began to gain more confidence. He wanted to be more athletic as well. He made the track team, which led to his placing a greater emphasis on nutrition and fitness.

Pedro flourished at New World Prep. He entered PRHS with a greater sense of himself. However, family conflicts did not subside. He blamed himself quite a bit for all of it. He ran away a number of times. Coming out as gay around this time did not reduce tensions at home. However, his mother was his rock. Pedro set modest expectations for himself. His mother was a home health aide, and he thought he would get a high school degree and follow in her path. A college education was outside of his family's experience. They had little understanding of it.

Fresh from his middle school success, Pedro started high school with his usual ebullience, getting along with others. He joined student government and track. His high school principal, Tim Gannon, noticed Pedro's natural leadership and civic abilities. Principal Gannon could see beyond Pedro's limited expectations. He immediately insisted that Pedro apply for the PRPLA program at Wagner. Pedro resisted mightily. "Mr. Gannon, I am not college material. I am not going to college. No one in my family even knows what that is." Principal Gannon insisted. He cajoled, harangued, and finally convinced Pedro to apply for one of the twelve spots. As we discussed earlier in chapter 5, the PRPLA program is a joint venture as part of the PRP. It requires three years of summer residency at Wagner, completion of a rigorous curriculum taught by tenured faculty members, and training in the theory and practice of democratic leadership, and it includes civic field placements. Upon completion of the program, PRPLA students receive a high school diploma and credit for a full semester of college credits.

Pedro fulfilled his promise to his mother. He not only joined the program and earned the scholarship to Wagner, but he excelled as a leader. He found his Wagner College undergraduate mentors, who mostly looked like him, to be remarkable role models. They introduced him to the necessary skill sets for college to help him succeed at the next level. They held endless group and individual counseling sessions where PRPLA students could open up about their fears, challenges, and personal experiences. They began to reset their goals, now less fearful of reaching well beyond what they knew.

Once at Wagner, Pedro applied for the Bonner Leaders Program. This is part of the Bonner Foundation's twenty-five-year-old national program for low-income students that emphasizes college readiness and civic leadership. In addition to a substantive leadership curriculum, Bonner leaders are required to complete 300 hours of service each year. The core principle of Bonner links learning, leadership, and service as part of an integrated pathway for a transformative education.

Pedro excelled in the program. He took on major leadership roles. While he became a college mentor to the PRPLA program at PRHS he also became part of what developed as the educational pipeline—discussed in earlier chapters—where elementary, middle, and high school cohorts were linked around a first-generation college prep and civic leadership program. His PRPLA education not only prepared him for college but helped him find purpose and resolve. Recently Pedro told me, "I didn't think I was good enough for college, but this changed my life."

Pedro was inspired by his mother. "I was so down and hurt, personally, when my mom was diagnosed with cancer. I needed to do more for her. She was my anchor. PRPLA and Wagner helped me find a common thread between my life and the community. I cried in the counseling sessions with my mentors. I found out in dialogues that I was not alone. Engagement and community gave me purpose to do more and be more."

Pedro is applying for graduate school in counseling. He wants to work with youngsters who are living the life he overcame. How many boys like him will he find and how many will he help find themselves? How many will he mentor to become leaders themselves, transforming the daily lives of residents in shadow communities? How many Pedros are out there with untapped potential for learning, for leadership, and for positive change? How many are ignored, pushed aside, and forgotten? How can American schools throw away so many young children before

American society fails? And how many colleges and universities can afford not to locate and educate the Pedros? How many would want them as loyal, ardent alumni and supporters?

Kellie Griffith, Student and Civic Professional

With blond hair and blue eyes, Kellie Griffith arrived at Wagner College from the far suburbs of Suffolk County, Long Island, as a freshman in 2010. Unlike Pedro Santiago, Kellie came from a more advantaged background. She, however, was not as privileged as some wealthy students. Her family is a middle-class suburban one with two lovely parents. Her father worked for a utility company and her mother was the family home worker. As you will see, however, Kellie and Pedro are two sides of the same fabric of social justice, engaged learning, and democratic transformation.

Like all entering Wagner students, Kellie was placed in the First-Year Program (FYP), which combines students into twenty-four-person cohorts. They enroll in a three-course learning community, which is organized around a central theme. Two of the courses are drawn from traditional academic disciplines, while the third course is a reflective tutorial (RFT) set in two separate sections, each with half of the LC students. The RFT focuses on the central theme and how the two disciplines are needed to properly engage it. The emphasis is on critical thinking, effective writing and communication skills, and direct field-based experience. Students are asked to integrate the text-based knowledge with the field-based learning. Often these LCs provide civic-based field experiences; most times, those civic engagements take place in Port Richmond. The FYP is one of the four spokes on the Wagner Plan for the Practical Liberal Arts.

From the very start, Kellie knew she wanted to be an elementary school teacher. Beginning in middle school, she loved her courses in Spanish. She chose a freshman LC that allowed her to combine her interests. This would begin her pathway to becoming a brilliant student, engaged teacher, and remarkably dedicated civic professional.

Kellie's field work took place in Port Richmond. She immediately was useful to the community because of her dual-language skills. She wanted to understand the community, its families, and its children. By sophomore year, she declared a dual major in Spanish and elementary education. As part of her civic work, she met a most remarkable young professional and very recent Wagner alumna, Samantha Siegel, director of the Center for Leadership and Community Engagement. Samantha recognized Kellie's commitment and began to place her in important sessions about Port Richmond. Kellie and a growing number of her friends found the work in Port Richmond becoming an identity for them. It intensified their desire to learn about language, culture, economics, and politics. Kellie and the other students needed to learn why the structure of political and economic authority produced the levels of poverty, racial discrimination, and limited opportunity in this neighborhood. What composite of cultural and global forces leads to the migration and ultimately exploitation of different peoples of the world? In short, their civic engagement with a community that was opening itself to them on a personal level proved to be the catalyst of their desire for a broad and deep education. With an endless thirst for new knowledge, they wanted to couple their campus-based learning with their field work. Through thorough interrogation and deep reflection, they began to formulate a more vivid meaning of what they were experiencing.

By her third year, Kellie was named a student fellow for education and college readiness as part of the administration of the PRP. She worked more deeply with the schools. For instance, every Friday afternoon the schools would assist immigrant children with their new language, English. Kellie would attend all parent-teacher conferences, assisting parents and teachers across their language barriers. She would attend all field trips. Her assistance to P.S. 19 proved invaluable. The impact on Kellie was indelible.

Kellie spent her last year in the senior program component of the Wagner Plan, combining a major capstone course over 100 hours of related field-based learning and a senior thesis or project. She completed her student teaching for the elementary degree, then applied for a Fulbright Scholarship. To be selected for this prestigious award, the applicant must be successful in a demanding internal competitive process and then an even more fierce national process. At that time, Wagner had only had one student selected to become a Fulbright Scholar—a recent science student who also was selected by the top five medical schools in the United States. Based on her academic achievement, her highly intelligent proposal, her appropriate skill set, particularly in language, and her brilliant interviews at Fulbright, Kellie was chosen for a scholarship to study and teach in Ecuador. The Fulbright Committee appreciated her experience, her study abroad in Costa Rica and Spain, and her volunteer work for Habitat for Humanity.

Kellie flourished in Ecuador at an early childhood center, teaching English. When her year was up, Kellie could pick or choose whatever prestigious American day school she wanted in beginning her teaching career. If she suddenly wanted a different career in business or such, her language skills, international experience, excellent academic record, and demonstrated leadership skills likely would have fetched a six-figure starting salary. Instead,

Kellie chose to return to Port Richmond and continue what she started. She was hired at P.S. 19 as a teacher of the lower grades. She recently told me, "I put very hard work into my education at Wagner and into Port Richmond. And they put a lot into me. It all became part of my identity. I was taught to build an antiracist, cross-cultural education for my students. I wanted to get right back to it."

After a combined five years at P.S. 19 and P.S. 22 in Port Richmond, Kellie recently relocated to a new elementary school in Jackson Heights in Queens, New York. When she left P.S. 22, Kellie visited every home of her 42 students to say goodbye and encourage them. As a dual-language teacher, Kellie says, "I see my little students in kindergarten or first graders coming into a world dominated by English speakers. It is so difficult to succeed in that environment. Much harder than a child like me would have had it. I want them to know that every child is valued and loved in my classroom."

Kellie employs an asset-minded educational approach to learning. She works with each child, emphasizing his or her strengths in building confidence in the learning process. This is so critical in a dual-language school setting that is educationally challenged. Kellie knew she wanted to expand her teaching effectiveness, so she chose a master's degree program at City College, part of CUNY, despite the fact that it required a four-hour round-trip commute while she was still working full-time at P.S. 22. She now is pursuing a second master's degree in global studies and urban education. She wants to keep building her teaching and her understanding of her students and their worlds so that she can become even more impactful. She told me, "Students are listening always. They hear the hatred and they see the conflicts. We all need to be there for them in their education and to nurture them to become leaders for a better world."

The impact of civic engagement and anchor partnerships work is clearly illustrated in Kellie's biography. We wish all children would have the advantage of a gifted, extraordinary, and caring teacher in their early years. Such teachers open doors into their young selves. They give confidence and build self-esteem. They foster a true love of learning through reading and doing. The fact that Kellie realizes her gifts are most important in the Port Richmonds and Jackson Heights of the world demonstrates that she is becoming a true model of a well-educated, ethical, and engaged civic professional.

Tim Gannon, Community Partner and High School Principal

Tim Gannon became principal of PRHS on Staten Island in 2005. He became one of the major leaders of the PRP over the next twelve years. I had the privilege of partnering with Tim over that time. After an initial meeting in my office, we decided I would come visit the high school. Having grown up in Brooklyn and sharing a lifetime with a dedicated educator, Carin Guarasci, I was not unfamiliar with high schools in poor inner-city communities. They usually suffered from an acute lack of resources, beleaguered faculty and staff, high levels of truancy, violence of all forms, racial conflicts, and very low institutional self-esteem. For most principals, just surviving the day without an extraordinary incident would be a welcome outcome.

These stereotypes framed my expectations on the first visit to PRHS. As I drove up to the modest building, just negotiating a parking spot was difficult. Security was present, and eventually I found a spot. I entered the building and immediately was stopped by a security guard at a front desk. I identified myself and suddenly a staff member appeared to escort me to the principal's office. As I ascended the staircase to the next floor, I immediately knew that this school broke many of those stereotypes. Virtually every wall and public area was decorated with vibrant posters of student achievement. One wall featured a student who won a chess tournament. Another wall showed a student who won a math competition. Turn to the left and a team was celebrating a victory, while yet other posters showed off elaborate celebrations of some major civic undertaking by the school. This went on until I reached Tim's office.

Soon after a short meeting to further our conversation about how to align the college's social capital and physical assets with the high school community, I was introduced to eight PRHS students. They were going to explain the school to me and then I would explain the college. I was accompanied by Samantha Siegel and other Wagner staff. The PRHS students announced that we would eat lunch in the principal's office and that it was prepared for us by their fellow students in the culinary program.

In short order, these students shared their educational hopes, fears, and dreams. They came from all sorts of backgrounds. They ranged from fourteen to sixteen years old. They were modest and sincere. Tim cleverly left us alone with them for periods of time so the students would conduct the meeting without his supervision. His confidence in letting them tell their own stories let us know that they had so much to offer. They knew so little, if anything, about college, but as college educators we could see their potential more than they could. It did not take much for the Wagner team to leave that session with unbridled determination to find a way to work with these students and with the PRHS community.

The reader needs to know that prior to Tim arriving at PRHS as principal, the most recent reputation of PRHS was quite low. The borough community perceived it as ranking at the bottom of the seven public high schools on Staten Island. It had suffered from racial incidents, violence, and ongoing ethnic conflicts among White, African American, and Mexican students. In Tim Gannon's own words, "We were the struggling school in a roughshod community. . . . We were the school with a struggling graduation rate that fought through bias that undocumented immigrants and minorities faced on a daily basis. . . . Schools were often closed in NYC in the early 2000s, and rumors always surrounded our future. . . . If any school on Staten Island was going to close, the rumor mills had our name."

Tim describes his staff and faculty as caring and dedicated. I know that his determination in confronting these difficult circumstances rallied them around a greater sense of mission. Transformative leaders do that. Privately, Tim felt on the defensive, and he was distracted and discouraged at times. Then we found each other—the college expanding its civic mission as an anchor partner and the high school offering an opportunity to discover this creative community and its adolescent children. In Tim's words again, "The Wagner College-PRP helped to change the self-esteem of an entire high school community, and an even larger neighborhood, and it certainly had the same impact on me."

Tim's supervisors at the New York City Department of Education (DOE) focused the majority of their professional conversations on raising achievement scores while Tim also wanted to discuss "the issues of bias, equity, and poverty that were also very real challenges to our students." Eventually, these latter issues came into vogue with the DOE. "I was no longer the only person in the room who felt that our students no longer should just settle for a high school degree as the zenith of their education," Tim said. The partnership gave credibility to his vision that "if we could change the defeatist culture of a local poor community through education, we could empower those learners to become the local leaders of tomorrow. . . . Richard and his staff and students were now my partner in battling poverty and bias. I had an entire college community who understood the value of my students and their families."

All of this energized Tim. He became even more of a leader and voice not only in the K–12 educational community on Staten Island but also in New York City. One example is illustrative. When we launched the first summer of PRPLA, the sophomore high school students were enrolled in the theory and practice of American democracy. In addition to the classics of American government, they were introduced to an asset management approach to understanding their own community. This was an essential part of their civic training. We used a critical text by John Kretzmann and John McKnight, *Building Communities from the Inside Out*, which explains that community progress is made by building out from the neighborhood's assets and not by focusing on the local social and economic pathologies.[2] The latter approach has framed so much of urban public policy in the past seventy-plus years, and obviously without much success. To this end, we asked the fifteen-year-old PRPLA students to literally map the assets of Port Richmond. Accordingly, they identified the churches, libraries, schools, and eventually the nonprofits, parks, and so on. Asset mapping became their new skill. At the end of the summer, they gave organized tours to their parents, relatives, and friends, all of whom had never thought of their neighborhood in this way.

As we progressed with building out the PRPLA program and a number of other initiatives around educational, health disparities, and cultural programming, Tim took the additional and daring step of applying for "community school" status for PRHS. No other school on Staten Island had this distinction. A school that receives it obtains greater resources. To be awarded, the applicant needed to demonstrate that the school would offer significant academic enhancements to the school population as well as provide significant physical and additional programming for the entire local community. Wagner College maintained two major spaces on-site at PRHS. One was the Wagner Raider Room, which was a year-round, five-day-a-week learning center for PRPLA students and a resource for all PRHS students. Programming included tutoring, counseling, college counseling, and a meeting space. The second was a professional development room allowing Wagner's Education faculty to work with PRHS faculty. We even taught master's degree courses on-site. In addition, Staten Island University Hospital opened up a medical office on-site as part of the partnership. Wagner's School of Nursing partnered with the PRHS Culinary Arts Program, and Wagner's Physician Assistant Program also added instruction and guidance.

Port Richmond was selected as a community school, the first one on Staten Island. This was a remarkable turnaround in perception. The mayor of New York and the New York chancellor of schools attended the ribbon-cutting ceremony. They visited the Wagner Raider Room and met with the PRPLA students.

There are some delightful moments to cherish in this work. One was a meeting of all the New York City principals and key staff from the chosen community schools. After proper introductions and a general orientation about this new designation, the DOE facilitator began by asking all of the principals to identify "asset mapping" and if any of them had ever done one. After a long, awkward silence, Tim Gannon, the principal of a school that is often overlooked on the usually ignored borough of Staten Island, perked up and said, "My sophomores did one at Wagner College last year. Would you like me to show you how it is done?"

Another indelible moment occurred when Tim was somewhere in Queens for a major New York City educational meeting. He received a call from his assistant principal regarding some routine business. He happened to ask if anything was going on that he should know. His assistant informed him that a particular student was delivering a baby. Always intense, Tim's blood pressure must have exploded. Things like this happen in poor neighborhood schools. "Baby . . . delivery . . . how, why?" Tim was very pleased finally to learn that the Wagner Physician Assistant Program's faculty and students had invited the PRPLA students who showed interest in a health career to visit their simulation lab. They were participating in a simulated birthing provided by an artificial patient and newborn, a scene that is quite vivid and realistic. From what I was told, Tim had a beer that night in the privacy of his kitchen. His wonderful wife, Carolyn, a high school educator at another Staten Island school, must have had a long laugh over that one.

Many Wagner faculty students were at the high school or in the community every day. Wagner started a van service to and from Port Richmond every day. Just their presence was uplifting for the community. The fact that a college was taking their children seriously was a source of hope. Wagner staff, students, and faculty would often eat in Maria's restaurant with the Mexican day workers. Many of our students spoke Spanish—or enough of it to communicate. All sorts of personal relationships began.

Tim Gannon led the conceptualization, design, and leadership for the educational pipeline that included the elementary, middle school, and high school alignment. He identified and cultivated three truly remarkable principals as partners, namely Nick Mele (I.S. 51), Anthony Cosentino (P.S. 21), and Tim's successor at PRHS, Andrew Greenfield. Along with Wagner staff, they have presented their pipeline work at national higher education conferences, which is rare in New York circles. They have become leaders in community school and anchor partnership presentations. Wagner maintains offices in all three schools with wraparound educational services and an integrated approach to academic achievement, civic engagement, and leadership development.

Tim is a model community partner. We shared many breakfasts at a local diner to make sure this was effective. We would discuss individual students, program dynamics, new funding sources, and next steps. We supported one another in this work. We widened the circle along the way. We were making sure the Mindys and Pedros were succeeding and that the Kellies and other college students were growing from their engagement. We depended on them and most importantly, we cherished the work of our faculty and staff. Tim says this "forever changed" his life.

Nyeema Watson, Administrator as Leader

Nyeema Watson is the associate vice chancellor for civic engagement at Rutgers University–Camden. Her personal story is a compelling example of the impact of anchor partnership. She is a national as well as campus leader for transformative civic engagement. Her journey started as a first-generation African American high school student and culminates to date as a major force for creating critical pathways for students with similar biographies. With her generous and professional leadership style, she oversees the highly regarded anchor work at the university.

A Camden native, she is the ninth of eleven children of two conscientious parents who had five children and adopted six more. She was one of the adoptees. "I am a woman of faith, but I don't believe in accidents. I am blessed that by whatever pathway my biological mother made it to this place, she was able to find my mother and father who raised me here [Camden, New Jersey]. I think just being in a city that at times has a beauty, but immense challenges, has made me who I am today." Now Nyeema is "Dr. Watson," having earned her doctorate at Rutgers University after previously earning her master's degree at the University of Pennsylvania.

While education was emphasized at home, a high school diploma was considered aspirational. Facing economic challenges with their family circumstances, both of Nyeema's parents had to drop out of middle school and care for siblings. In spite of her family having little to no knowledge about college, Nyeema had seen popular television images of African American youngsters aspiring to attend historically Black colleges. With that small amount of familiarity, she set her sights on a college degree. She had little assistance in acquiring the requisite information about college applications and the admissions process. She was an academically successful student in high school, and she was active as a peer leader, as the drum major in the school band, and as a volunteer in community service. Even though Nyeema had what would appear to be, at minimum, an attractive profile for most colleges, her high school social worker advised her to forego any college aspirations and attend beauty school.

In the spring of her senior year of high school, Nyeema found an ally, a young, suburban White teacher who casually asked her where she intended to attend college. When Nyeema told her she wasn't likely to attend, her teacher provided critical support in demystifying the process. She assisted her with college applications and FAFSA paperwork and met with Nyeema's parents. She could attend the local college as a commuter student. Two weeks before classes started at Rutgers–Camden, Nyeema signed up for classes and attempted to register. When she was told she needed to post her first semester's tuition, she collapsed into tears. Her family did not have the resources for a semester's tuition. Viewing all of this, the director of financial aid and a counselor sorted it all out, and Nyeema's college career began.

Similar to Pedro Santiago, Nyeema's fortunes were changed dramatically. Opportunities would be available to her that she would not have had without her determination to rise above expectations and without the good work of a few allies. What is significantly different in the two cases is that Nyeema's good fortune was a result of serendipity and luck while Pedro's was the outcome of intentionality. His came from a designed program to interrupt the fate that was likely to stem from institutional racism, economic inequality, and educational apartheid, namely the PRP and its PRPLA program. Nyeema's fortune was more dependent on the goodness of a teacher and a few understanding administrators who just happened to be on the scene at the right time. Today, Nyeema's role at Rutgers University–Camden is to sustain and expand the intentionality that more Nyeemas and Pedros get the opportunity to realize their inherent intelligence, creativity, and leadership qualities.

Nyeema recently told me, "I still have students at my alma mater who have the desire to get to college but have no idea of the process or who haven't even been allowed to imagine themselves as college material so they don't even think about higher education, or they have been told college is not for them." She went on to say, "There are students who, like myself, graduate at the top of their class but have not had the educational rigor to hit the ground running once they get into college. We know what happens with some of those students. They get frustrated and drop out." Nyeema holds a different expectation for them. She leads the community-based learning programs that include early grade tutoring to support grade-level or advanced reading, college awareness, civic engagement, and all the experiences gained with university-school partnerships. She is, in fact, a remarkable role model.

In the previous chapter, I presented the successful and comprehensive anchor work underway at Rutgers–Camden. It is making a palpable difference in the lives of students with similar profiles to Nyeema's. She views this work as an imperative for higher education. She urges and supports Rutgers faculty members to get involved and remain committed to the community-based learning courses, the university's civic-oriented research, and making students aware of the realities of inequality and institutionalized racism laced throughout Camden and the nation. "We all can't drive onto campus and just ignore the inequalities that we pass by," she said.

Nyeema always is focused on student success. She knows that her own story could have turned out so differently. She is rigorous about her work and that of the university. Is it realizing its maximum impact? Are enough faculty and staff involved? Will the university stay the course? She quotes Dr. Martin Luther King Jr.: "Shallow understanding from people of good will is more frustrating than absolute misunderstanding from people of ill will." She goes on to ask her national as well as local colleagues "to be willing to ask if we are recreating inequity on our campuses or if we are even truly focused on inequity? We always must be willing to dig deep, truly reflect, and begin to rethink how we engage."

Margarita Sánchez and Sarah Donovan, Faculty in Action

Two of the finest faculty members that I had the privilege of working alongside, Margarita Sánchez and Sarah Donovan, are excellent models for the way in which anchor partnerships shape educators' scholarship, teaching, and personal lives. Both are transformative educators who continue to dramatically affect the lives of so many in forgotten neighborhoods in the United States and abroad. They are major agents for change in the PRP and in the Oaxaca town of San Jeronimo, the original homeland of the Mexican immigrants in the partnership.

Sarah grew up in a small town in Maine while Margarita was raised in Medellín, Colombia. Sarah studied philosophy and Spanish in college. She had the opportunity to study abroad in Ecuador, and the program fostered her love of other cultures. She completed a very traditional curriculum for her PhD in philosophy at Villanova University. Margarita studied journalism at a college in Colombia. She always had an acute interest in social justice, but the climate for journalists in Medellín was quite dangerous. She immigrated to New York and found employment teaching in ESL programs. Eventually she completed her PhD in literature at Rutgers University, and she retained her passion for assisting the powerless in gaining their own voice.

Both women found their way to full-time, tenure-track teaching positions at Wagner College. By then, the Wagner Plan for the Practical Liberal Arts was well established. They both were enlisted for teaching in Wagner's FYP. Sarah admits that her traditional training in philosophy was removed completely from any familiarity or knowledge of how to incorporate experiential learning into her teaching, which is a defining piece of the FYP. She had to translate metaphysics and social philosophy into the concrete realities of everyday life in Port Richmond. She recently told me that her salvation was in meeting and pairing with Margarita as part of their FYP Learning Community.

Conversely, Margarita found the FYP's experiential learning component the perfect opportunity for her to incorporate her interest in social justice into her courses on Spanish literature. She discovered Port Richmond and its predominantly struggling undocumented Mexican population. Relating their experience to her own as a relatively recent immigrant, Margarita volunteered significant time at the local nonprofit El Centro del Immigrante. Under the founding leadership of an important civic partner for Wagner in helping to form the PRP, Gonzalo Mercado found key ways to include Margarita in assisting day laborers and their families in negotiating any number of everyday challenges. Along with Tim Gannon, Gonzalo provided critical leadership in framing the partnership. He later would leave El Centro to found a successful worker cooperative, La Colmena, in Port Richmond. Margarita was a founding and continuing board member of the cooperative and remains a key ally.

Not only did Sarah teach in all three levels of the Wagner Plan learning communities, but she also became a fixture teaching the high school PRPLA students who were living on Wagner's campus in the summer. They would take her course, Philosophy 203, Social Philosophy: Ethics and Society, for college credit. They would employ the concepts of the traditional Western philosophers in studying issues of race, racism, and education in their own neighborhood. Students would compare and contrast the traditional texts in sorting through the viability and appropriateness for a variety of solutions. Sarah would use a case study method where theory and experience were explored in class and in written work. Not surprisingly, one of her memorable students was Pedro Santiago.

The anchor work became an important part of Sarah's professional scholarship. She was building her own pedagogical practice with issues of equity, diversity, and inclusion. She was quite innovative and successful in combining the case method with direct civic and experiential learning. This led to her coediting two important books on this subject.[3] Both were inspired by her teaching in the PRPLA program.

Margarita collaborated with Gonzalo in creating a breathtaking international venture that would help reunite the undocumented Mexican families in Port Richmond with their Mexican relatives, many of whom were unable to be with their families because their legal status in the United States prevented them from crossing back to Oaxaca. The U.S. government accepted the transnational program, allowing Oaxaca residents to visit the United States as cultural ambassadors if a sponsoring educational or cultural institution requested and accounted for the residents' visas. This would mean that many individuals with whom we were working in Port Richmond could now see their parents, siblings, and children whom they had not seen for years.

When presented with the opportunity to partner with Margarita and Gonzalo, I immediately authorized Wagner College as a sponsor institution. The accepted Mexican applicants would receive visas ranging from a week to a month. They would perform native songs, dances, and other cultural offerings for our campus and local community while also being reunified with their loved ones. I would host a traditional Oaxacan meal and reception for them in the large presidential suite at the college. I would invite our involved students, faculty, and staff to join the Port Richmond and Oaxacan families. These were some of the most moving moments of my life.

The Oaxaca's San Jeronimo community is rural and poor, with a native non-Spanish ethnicity. They speak a separate dialect. They are not familiar with urban, postindustrial America. This was a very long and challenging journey for them, but reunification with families meant everything to them. To those of us at the college and in the partnerships, we understood the significance for our neighbors in finding their "lost" relatives. Margarita was the driving force. We all learned so much from her unrelenting determination to see this happen. Over the years, we had at least four such reunification visits.

In particular, one visit stands out to me. I will not use the real name of the undocumented Port Richmond person involved. This wonderful, humble woman in her midlife was forced to flee San Jeronimo because her life was in danger. She was a victim of brutal domestic violence and rape as a young woman. She left her three children, ages three to seven, with her mother. She fled to the United States and landed in Port Richmond. Her intention was to earn some money, return to Mexico, and restart her family with more resources. Life changed as a year away turned into several years. She held all sorts of jobs and sent money back to Mexico. Nearly twenty years passed, and the moment of reunification came in my office when one of her children had just graduated from college in Mexico. The power of this moment was emotionally intense. The harshness of the family's lives was hard to take in.

The woman and others will be the subject of a forthcoming book by coauthors Margarita and Sarah on the entire transnational program. It will discuss the dynamics and lives of the two communities separated by physical borders but part of the international division of labor now re-sorting itself in the face of global capitalism and climate change. Margarita and Sarah are scholars whose academic scholarship is rigorous, civic, and mightily impactful in presenting the human side of global economic systems, inequality, cultural bigotry, and the foundations of privileged societies.

Their work isn't limited to their scholarship. Clearly their teaching is equally impactful. They have shaped and are shaping the lives of students and families across the economic and cultural divisions that surround all of us. In addition to the Pedros and Kellies that they have influenced, there are so many others. For instance, Jazmin Diaz, who graduated from Wagner in 2017 as an anthropology major, was a student of theirs. As a Bonner leader, she mentored many of the PRPLA students. In her junior and senior years, she volunteered and studied Port Richmond and the workers at La Colmena. She worked intimately with the Reunification Program on both sides of the border. After graduating, she took a staff position at La Colmena and helped organize a daycare cooperative of the Mexican women in Port Richmond. It was a successful cooperative offering daycare services to the entire borough of Staten Island. Today, Jazmin is a scholarship student in the master's program in urban planning at the University of Pennsylvania. She will serve for five years in the American Foreign Service with the U.S. Agency for International Development. As an alumna of Wagner College, the Wagner Plan, and the PRP, and as a student of Margarita Sanchez and Sarah Donovan, Jazmin Diaz will pay it all forward. She, too, came from an underserved background to an anchor college, and she will find her way in the world as a force for equity, diversity, and inclusion.

Margarita and Sarah are models of the teacher, scholar citizen ideal. They form the bedrock of "the good college." Many others like them are spread around the nation, performing this type of transformative teaching and scholarship. They demonstrate how civic engagement and anchor institution practice shape an impactful, generative academic career and personal lives of significance.

Liz Harrington, Civic Professional

In May 2013, I was hurrying between the annual board of trustees meeting and a number of other ceremonial events that preceded commencement ceremonies the following day. I was asked to stop in for an appearance at the School of Nursing "pinning," the recognition for the graduating nurses as they entered their profession. It has a valued history at nursing schools. This one was taking place at a family-filled auditorium in the middle of campus. Given my schedule, the dean of nursing expected that I would offer congratulations and then excuse myself in order to get to my next set of meetings.

I followed the script, except I thought it would be disrespectful to leave because a student speaker would follow me. I stayed on for what I thought would be a few extra minutes. Liz Harrington was the undergraduate chosen to speak for her peers and the nursing faculty. I had met her a few times during her senior year, and I knew she was a mature and serious student leader. I sat back with some interest, but I was not prepared for these remarks.

Liz began her speech by discussing that becoming an effective health-care professional, particularly a nurse, required cultural competencies in order to practice in the ethnically and racially diverse settings where health-care professionals would be assigned. At Wagner, she learned about diversity in her courses and in her deep dive into civic work. She was committed to community health and patient advocacy. She went on to discuss how she spent her entire senior year interning in Port Richmond at El Centro del Immigrante, working with undocumented Mexican immigrants with very rural backgrounds.

She described the community's impoverished condition, which she found more troubling than she had expected. She found day laborers without insurance. She encountered men sharing extremely cramped sleeping arrangements in substandard housing where residents could only have access to a bed for eight hours, rotating to others because there were so many occupants. She found that the men's diets were nutritionally deficient. They had little access to basic hygiene. They often were not paid for their completed work since those who employed them knew that they were undocumented and vulnerable to legal authorities. Fear of deportation permeated the undocumented community. They shied away from hospitals.

At El Centro, Liz focused on health screenings and basic health education. She also advocated for better conditions and resources. She was experiencing in real time the immense health disparities that she was taught to expect. She said that her fellow interns "discovered that they needed to educate themselves about the depth of health issues in Port Richmond and the monumental health challenges." They found out about the high rates of illness from cancer, obesity, asthma, and depression. They researched the relationship between poor nutrition and depression. Liz prioritized sessions on nutrition, healthy eating habits, and hygiene. The workers' health screenings turned up alarmingly low blood pressure, likely due to excessive manual labor. Workers regularly put in twelve-hour days.

"At first at El Centro, the local residents felt threatened by the Wagner nursing students, but after many visits they began to share their health issues with us," Liz said. "Because we spoke Spanish with them, they eventually opened their arms to us." She gave one vivid example of a man who was sleeping on a cold floor and had not eaten for two days. "He complained of abdominal pain. . . . We kept talking with him in Spanish and smiling at him, making him feel safe. We were getting appropriate help for him. He had tears in his eyes, and he said, 'God bless you.'" Liz went on to speak of other sessions where the students taught the El Centro participants about basic dental care and related issues. They would demonstrate dental care for the residents and sometimes they received puzzling looks. They learned to trust each other and laugh together as the students gave these abandoned families the respect and dignity that any Wagner-educated nurse learned to provide in the diversity courses and campus dialogues.

Then Liz turned to the larger meaning of an education that integrated the liberal arts and sciences with professional education. This is what we called the practical liberal arts at Wagner. Liz's liberal arts and sciences faculty taught her about the breadth and depth of the human experience. They introduced her to diverse cultures and historical periods. They prepared her to engage difference, complexity, nuance, and, most important, ambiguity. Liz's Nursing School faculty members taught her how to be excellent in her field, maintain very high standards of care, and practice with integrity and ethical regard for her patients.

In closing her speech, Liz thanked her faculty members for giving her a love of learning and being open to discovering the new and different. They prepared her to be a leader in health care. Then she said what I could only have hoped she would say. She noted that she had two faculties, arts and sciences and nursing, but her other faculty was the Port Richmond community. "They taught me so much. . . . They were my teachers, too. . . . They taught us to reach beyond ourselves . . . to respect all differences and embrace our own abilities to be successful in restoring the health of our patients. We learned to work for the elimination of health disparities. . . . Wagner fostered our love of people and nursing." She finished by saying in both Spanish and English, "To the men and women of Port Richmond, let the road rise up to meet you, may the wind always be at your back, may the sun always shine on your face, may the rains soften your fields, and until we meet again, may God hold you in his hands." This was truly a remarkable moment for Liz, her classmates, the assembled faculty, and families.

For me, it was a defining moment of the power of this work. It demonstrated how work in anchor partnerships leads to a fuller education where the breadth of the liberal arts is married to the professional arts and where text, experience, and reflection dramatically increase learning in its fullest form. Liz concluded by saying, "To my classmates, listen to your patients' hearts and then listen to your own with compassion, intelligence, knowledge, and dedication."

When she was an undergraduate, Liz Harrington completed important medical missions to La Candelaria, Mexico and Port-au-Prince, Haiti. She graduated, easily passed her licensing exam, and began her career in the emergency room as a trauma nurse for seven and a half years in Brooklyn, New York. Along the way she completed her master's degree, and she attained the nurse practitioner certification. To no one's surprise, she was on the front line in New York City during the COVID pandemic. In addition to her continuing employment with the Northwell Health System, Liz volunteered for additional COVID work and chose Port Richmond. Similar to Kellie Griffith and Jazmin Diaz, she wanted to finish her commitment to the community she came to love and the neighborhood that served as her other faculty. She is now starting a doctoral program in nursing. She will continue with her short-term global medical missions. I have told her that I see her as a dean of a major school of nursing and from there it would not surprise me to discover that she is leading the entire university. She sets the standard for civic professionalism.

Summary

In this chapter, I chose particular profiles to demonstrate the impact of the civic work on the highlighted individuals as well as others. I could easily have selected another thirty individuals, but that would be another book by itself.

For instance, you did not get to meet remarkable civic engagement directors such as Arlette Cepeda, who led Wagner's Center for Leadership and Community Engagement. Arlette is not only a dynamic leader, but she is a resident of Port Richmond and a parent of both a PRHS student and a Wagner College student. An artist by training and Dominican by ethnicity, Arlette combined her personal biography with those of her neighborhood residents, her college students, and Bonner Leaders. Through this work, she has played a significant role on the national level as well.

You did not meet Jarrid Williams, an African American student, who came to Wagner as a talented Division I football player but woefully under-prepared as a college student. Like those students that Nyeema Watson mentors in Camden, Jarrid could easily have dropped out of college. His civic work saved him. He found purpose and meaning. He lost his stutter. He graduated on time. A shy young man as an underclassman, by senior year he was giving speeches about equity, diversity, and racial justice. He is now a teacher, undoubtedly changing lives that would be ignored or shunned.

You did not meet Leo Schuchert, who now is a director for civic engagement at Trinity College in Connecticut. He was one of the most impressive college mentors I have ever observed. He helped so many students like Jarrid find their voice and their purpose. Nor did I tell you about the remarkable Anthony Tucker Bartley, another African American male, who came to play football and found so much meaning in his love of science and the need to extend into the civic realm. He is graduating from Harvard Medical School and already is celebrated for his work in the Boston neighborhoods that mirror Port Richmond.

There are so many stories of truly transformative administrators, faculty members, and students from hundreds of colleges and universities. Their biographies conform to the ones I chose for this book. They all exemplify the remarkable educational and civic impact of anchor institution practice.

Notes

1. All of these profiles are in part based on direct interviews.
2. See John P. Kretzmann and John McKnight, *Building Communities from The Inside Out: A Path Toward Finding and Mobilizing a Community's Assets* (Chicago: ACTA Publications, 1993).
3. See Stephanie L. Burrell Storms, Sarah K. Donovan, and Theodora P. Williams, eds., *Equity, Diversity, and Inclusion (EDI): Innovation and Collaboration Across Disciplines* (New York: Rowman & Littlefield, 2020); Burrell Storms, Donovan, and Williams, eds., *Teaching Through Challenges for Equity, Diversity, and Inclusion* (New York: Rowman & Littlefield, 2020).

8

ANCHOR PARTNERSHIPS
AND COMMUNITY IMPACT

In general, universities and colleges maintain a significant economic and social impact on their local communities. Most provide relevant data on their respective websites with the intent of informing state and local governments of their economic impact. Private nonprofit institutions present these data to public officials and taxpayers to demonstrate their positive impact in lieu of paying property taxes. Public institutions rely on the same strategies in building public support for their local and state nontax status.

Despite higher education institutions' local and state economic imprint, some often miss the more critical point. The fiscal practices of these institutions can be significantly inferior to their local impact if, in fact, their hiring, purchasing, and spending policies are allocated outside of the region or city and not aligned with the needs and priorities of their indigenous communities. Reversing this approach is one of the central goals of anchor partnerships. The larger the university and the network of partners, the greater the impact on local class and racial inequality. When the fiscal aspects of the anchor partnership are integrated into the community with educational, health, and social goals, the result is increased probability for neighborhood equity and transformation.

Toward this end, Ted Howard, Gar Alperovitz, and their colleagues founded the Democracy Collaborative with the intent of forming "a research center for democratic renewal, increased civic participation, and community revitalization."[1] The center provides advisory services to local government, foundations, and anchor institutions. It supports the anchor institution approach to community university and neighborhood partnerships. It conceives of its work as building community wealth in advancing a more dynamic, fair, and just economy and a more inclusive society.

Toward that end, the Democracy Collaborative created the Anchor Institution Dashboard. Primarily, this is a vehicle for a roster of best practices in maintaining a successful anchor partnership, collecting and assessing critical outcomes data, and demonstrating the significant influence of anchor partnerships in creating community prosperity. Naturally, the data are specific to the particular anchor partnerships and they don't present a clear national profile of this work. Nevertheless, I find the Democracy Collaborative's research important and helpful in pressing the case for the civic imperative and promoting the dual goals of renewing higher education's civic mission and advancing the democratic transformation of shadow neighborhoods.

Examples of Anchor Impact

While university-neighborhood partnerships are comprehensive in scope, universities find that committing to a strategic alignment of purchasing, hiring, and building practices is the most visible way to demonstrate positive community outcomes. This is the first step in the transformation of neighborhoods. For some higher education anchor institutions, this constitutes the bulk of their commitment. In this book, I have argued for the more comprehensive partnerships that touch all aspects of the core relationships in shadow neighborhoods as well as the academic and institutional dimensions of the campus.

As one example of the full measure of aligning university fiscal practice to privilege the local community, the FY 2020 Economic and Social Impact Report of the University of Pennsylvania (UPenn) demonstrates the depth of this approach.[2] By prioritizing hiring, purchasing, and direct expenditures, the university had a significant effect on these three areas. The study identified the following results for the City of Philadelphia: $15 billion of total activity, support for 80,150 jobs, allocation of $9.1 billion in wages, and $272 million in local taxes. The report cited specific outcomes deriving from the UPenn Civic Engagement and Social Impact practice. It listed $1.7 million spent from the UPenn's Way Campaign, $304 million in underfunded Medicaid funds underwritten, and $135.9 million in physical training support. For West Philadelphia, which is within the institution's educational anchor work, the report lists $27 million in direct support to the area's neighborhoods. Overall, the university assessed its annual civic engagement impact as $46 million, including 15,600 faculty, students, and staff engaging in 344,000 hours of service. They touched an estimated 718,000 Philadelphians through programs in public education, health, community development, and quality-of-life areas. Overall, it is evident that a major research university maintains a significant footprint on the local community. As more of it becomes strategically aligned with an anchor partnership and the local community of need, this one fiscal dimension provides a wellspring of new resources and opportunities for ignored and economically challenged communities. But of course, this is one part of a comprehensive democratic transformative partnership. In the longer run, the educational pipelines that can be created will prove decisive. It is the access to college learning and credentials that will allow personal and family lives to be changed dramatically. This becomes the pathway to generations of new, educated civic leaders across the professions, within these neighborhoods and across the nation. UPenn has been working at that form of civic engagement for the past thirty years.

Drexel University in Philadelphia is dedicated to the same model. In the past eight years, it has had solid results to share. The university has attempted to increase minority hiring, job access, and training, and expand the number of successful local businesses. With the help of the Annie E. Casey Foundation, Drexel created a comprehensive civic profile in direct practice, aligned spending, and increased local leadership capacity.[3]

I will offer three specific results of anchor partnerships' impacts on their local communities. Johns Hopkins University is located in Baltimore. As we have discussed earlier in this book, the depth of poverty and violence in that city is one of the worst among all of the nation's large cities. The leadership of the university addressed these problems through the anchor model by specifically focusing its hiring, purchasing, and building practices to support economic growth in the inner city.[4] In the three years from 2016 to 2019, the university and its health system hired more than one thousand city residents and spent $54 million more than the baseline year of 2015 in its support of local vendors. It increased its building expenditures with local providers by more than 23 percent in this same period. The president of the university and the CEO of the health system cite the success of this new initiative. The impact on minority business and employment is significant.

Tulane University is another model of a citywide anchor institution approach to economic and civic renewal. Devastated by Hurricane Katrina in August 2005, New Orleans appeared to be beyond repair. The university was totally flooded and closed for four months in the wake of the complete destruction of numerous buildings. Before Katrina, Tulane was the largest private employer in New Orleans. Afterward, it was the city's single largest employer. President Scott Cowan led his university to embrace the challenge of restoring his institution by having it be a central and ongoing force in the economic and civic life of New Orleans. The undergraduate curriculum refocused on experiential learning and civic participation in partnership with local schools, health providers, and business and public officials. In its recent report, *Powering New Orleans and Louisiana: The Economic and Social Impact of Tulane University*, the university cites an overall economic infusion of $3.4 billion into the state, with the largest share spent in the city of New Orleans. It has made $143 million of capital investments in New Orleans, supporting more than 700 new jobs as well. Local hiring, purchasing, and building expenditures are joined with dedicated civic engagement throughout campus life and mission. Tulane University partnered with 165 local agencies. The campus population provides 750,000 service hours. Its partnership with the City of New Orleans supports 19,535 jobs in the surrounding neighborhoods.

Temple University, another Philadelphia institution, maintains a partnership in the northern sector of the city. The Lenfest North Philadelphia Workforce Initiative focuses on the "earning potential of local communities by providing job training and career readiness programs for sustainable employment."[5] The university is allied with twenty community partners serving the unemployed, underemployed, and underpaid. It works with youth and adults, returning citizens, veterans, English language learners, immigrants, and those with disabilities. In its Lenfest Annual Report for 2019–2020, the measured impact is significant. Temple University spends $2.6 million in workforce development, serving more than 1,700 participants in twelve workforce development projects in North Philadelphia.

There are many other examples of higher education's economic impact throughout the United States. For instance, the University of Houston is part of the Third Ward Initiative to elevate that struggling minority neighborhood economically, educationally, in health care, and in the arts and culture. This is similar to Wagner College's PRP on Staten Island. For instance, the university's education programs seek to increase academic performance in reading readiness in lower grades and improve graduation and college attendance rates at the higher end.[6] Weber State University in Ogden, Utah, is a leading partner in sectoral anchor networks organized around health care and health disparities. Intermountain Healthcare is actually part of a larger coalition that not only integrates a variety of health providers and institutions but also involves the City of Ogden, the local schools in the Ogden School District, Ogden Technical College, Weber State University, and a number of local nonprofit organizations.[7]

These measurable outcomes provide partial data on the overall impacts on neighborhood and university revitalization. Much of the effect is qualitative. Forgotten and invisible communities suffer from a paucity of models and stories of personal and collective success. In a sense, expectations are low and dreams are deferred—in some cases, feared. As much as the measurable evidence affirms progress and can reveal defeats, the stories embedded in the lives of community partners are more revealing of the full potential for such comprehensive and democratically organized partnerships. Next, I will turn to these success stories.

The Human Face of Community Impact

The impact on the anchor partnerships is exemplified in the civic and personal biographies of community participants. I will share a few from the PRP. Each one presents an indelible signature of engaged democratic work. The biographies demonstrate the various ways that anchor partnerships reshape perceptions, expectations, neighborhood visibility, and self-agency.

Gonzalo Mercado

Gonzalo Mercado, director of transnational institutions, The National Day Laborer Network, is a force of nature within the Port Richmond community. In 2006, he was the founding director of El Centro Del Immigrante, a local nonprofit established to aid the large number of undocumented Mexican immigrants that were relocating to Staten Island at the turn of the century. These new neighbors lived in desperate fear of authority and were regularly exploited as day laborers working at the mercy of local construction and landscaping employers. Often, they were not paid after a long day of work or they were shortchanged. As undocumented residents, they had no recourse to legal authorities, courts, or other forms of redress. Sometimes they would be picked up on street corners in the early morning, taken to job sites— even across bridges and state lines—where they worked for twelve hours, and then were not paid. It was not unusual for them to find themselves without transportation to return home to their families. The Reverend Terry Troia, the leader of the largest antipoverty organization on Staten Island, Project Hospitality, founded El Centro. It was dedicated to improving the lives of these workers and their families, initially by gaining fair employment practices and just compensation.

El Centro was the first community partner for Wagner College's anchor efforts. It became one of the lead organizations in the PRP. Gonzalo was our first community partner. His collaboration proved invaluable in helping to introduce the community to Wagner. His leadership expanded the scope of the partnership, and together, the Wagner civic engagement team grew immensely in its understanding of these new residents, their culture, and their legacy. Gonzalo nurtured the strong relationships between local residents and the campus participants. Often, through community work, they formed mutual friendships that were built around the genuine needs and mutual interests of one another. As an immigrant from Chile during its brutal military dictatorship, Gonzalo relocated to New York City and was immediately taken by its social and cultural diversity. He enjoyed the personal and political openness of its everyday life. He became a citizen and later found his calling in addressing the situation of the undocumented Staten Island Mexicans. This has expanded to his international work with the diaspora of Latino immigrants spread throughout the advanced nations.

When I interviewed Gonzalo for this book, I asked him to identify the key outcomes and overall impact of the PRP on our local Staten Island neighborhood. He immediately pointed to four markers. First, he pointed to the importance of the college's recognition of this community that was largely invisible to the bulk of Staten Island's nearly five hundred thousand residents. Given Wagner's long history in the borough and its favorable local reputation, Gonzalo stressed the important effect of the college's publicly announced partnership agreement with the neighborhood, and particularly, the undocumented community. "No one else wanted to see or work with them, but Wagner invited them to the table," he said. To Gonzalo, this legitimized the immigrant community during a period of harsh and mean-spirited political rhetoric toward the undocumented community. The impact of merely gaining recognition was critical to the welfare, standing, and internal cohesion of this community. In poor neighborhoods, the absence of allies only underscores the political disempowerment baked into economic, social, and racial inequality. To paraphrase author Ralph Ellison in his iconic novel, *Invisible Man*, "responsibility rests upon recognition, and recognition is a form of agreement."[8] To Gonzalo, Wagner's recognition was a necessary first step that led to participation of the community partners and residents in the PRP.

The second impact for the community that Gonzalo was, of course, the significant access to new resources. Suddenly, young children and their families had greater opportunities in schoolwork, language tutoring, health-care practices, and access to something completely new and strange to them, a college campus and its many engaged students. In addition, Wagner College opened its campus facilities to this community, providing some educational, recreational, and friendship opportunities. Gonzalo cites the welcoming of the reunited international families with their undocumented Port Richmond relatives as a major moment of respect. On their immediate arrival in town from their rural Mexican villages, these travelers and their local relatives were feted to a warm and delightful dinner on campus with Wagner students, faculty, and administrators in the president's large office. Gonzalo said for almost all of them, it was their first time in a White person's home.

Third, he pointed to the benefits that the partnership offered in networking the community to so many of the local leaders, organizations, and businesses. Its previous network consisted of some nonprofit organizations and social workers. Later, its networks expanded to K–12 school leaders, college officials, elected office holders, hospital administrators, a range of significant nonprofit organizations, and local bank foundations.

Fourth, the connection between college students and Port Richmond youth proved invaluable. Not only were the direct services important to educational success in all levels of the K–12 schools, but the college students also became models in building and fortifying the aspirations of these young Black and Brown students. In addition to the Mexican youth, African and African American students in Port Richmond were now working with college students who looked like them. Very often, the encouragement and knowledge of the college students made the difference in building self-esteem and resiliency in K–12 students who had no other reference points for college attendance and success.

Gonzalo went on to describe a number of examples of direct community benefits from the partnership, but I found those cited previously the most important because they highlighted one of the potential roles of the established anchor partner, transferring its social standing and reputation and sharing it with its neighborhood partners. This is not a paternalistic gesture but rather the benefit of a democratically organized set of relationships where reciprocity, respect, and genuine collaborative practice lead to a mutual sharing of resources and assets. In a world beset by inequality, discrimination, and racism, successful partnerships rebalance the social equation.

The Three Principals: Anthony, Nick, and Andrew

The core of the educational pipeline in Port Richmond rests on the shoulders of three remarkable school principals. Anthony Cosentino is the principal at P.S. 21, an elementary school. Nick Mele is the principal of I.S. 51, an intermediate or middle school. Andrew Greenfield is the current principal of Port Richmond High School (PRHS). He worked with Tim Gannon, the former PRHS principal whom you met in a previous chapter. Each one is an exceptional leader. Through the pipeline, they have become professional colleagues and close friends. This is a rarity in the New York City public school system. Collectively, their vision, intelligence, caring, and resiliency are as inspiring as they are effective. They have built a pipeline that follows students from pre-K through high school, with the expectation of college acceptance and success for youngsters. Each school maintains an academic and leadership academy, respectively, with Wagner College. Each academy also stresses civic engagement in its neighborhood as part of the leadership development program. The express intent for each academy is preparation for college and for intercultural and inclusive democratic citizenship.

I interviewed each principal separately for this book. I have worked closely with each one, and together, we participated in presentations about the pipeline at national educational conferences on several occasions. They are outstanding leaders who are held in high esteem by their faculties, assistant principals, administrators, and most of all by their students and their families. Each became deeply immersed this past year in the challenges presented by the COVID-19 virus. They encountered long lapses of no in-person schooling and suffered physical and health tolls on their families and their own staffs. The virus has had a highly disproportionate impact on poor communities nationally, and Port Richmond is no exception. Andrew Greenfield reported to me that in the high school, with a population of approximately fifteen hundred students, thirteen parents have died from COVID-19 this year. One of his students lost both parents within a week of each other.

Andrew identified a number of community benefits from the PRP. As a graduate of the high school, he has a historical understanding of the community. He cites the major changes as the elevation of knowledge about attending college and access to a college education. In his time at PRHS, college was not a topic of interest. The expectation was that students would seek manual labor or entry-level jobs or join the military. Some would try for civil service employment or acceptance into the city's police, fire, or sanitation units. Andrew told me that, at present, college is an accepted part of the expectations for so many more of his high school students. They and their parents are quite aware of why college is important, how they need to prepare themselves, and how and where to seek financial assistance to support their educational plans. This is quite a change.

Andrew credits the PRP's continuous messaging, campus exposure, and direct educational services for this new social aspiration. He cited two other impacts of the partnership. He believes the Port Richmond neighborhood has much greater self-consciousness and civic pride. It is a real place and not merely an afterthought. As a result, Andrew said, there are more watchful eyes to make it a safer community. In the past ten years, he has noticed a real difference in students' personal safety. Previously, it was not safe to walk home from school. Now it is.

Finally, and quite importantly, PRHS has witnessed enrollment growth. Not long ago, it was regarded as a failing school. Some expected that it would be closed. It was known as unsafe, fraught with racial violence and high attrition rates. With the dawn of the Bloomberg administration, children could choose to apply to any school in New York City. They were no longer assigned to the high school in their neighborhood. This policy was put in place to spur competition among principals for funding. Andrew cites the PRP and high school's intimate relationship with Wagner College as a major attraction for families and middle schoolers choosing to attend PRHS.

Nick Mele is a dynamic educator. He is a high-energy personality with an acute emphasis on excellence at every level. He supports his faculty and staff with extra resources through grants and the local government's discretionary funding. He is totally dedicated to his middle school and the local community. He realized early on in his leadership role that too many I.S. 51 graduates encountered difficulty in high school. There were myriad reasons for the lack of success, but when Tim Gannon, then principal of PRHS, approached him about forming a relationship with his high school by joining the partnership with Wagner College, they invented the pipeline.

Nick believed that one key to unlocking the fuller potential of his middle school students was increasing expectations. This required creating a self-consciousness about building a future for themselves as they entered his school in the sixth grade. This would necessitate the full support of their families. In poor neighborhoods, everyday life is a struggle and consequently, time horizons get condensed. To expand them, the engagement with civic work and with positive college role models more likely would open up new experiences and greater personal possibilities. But the challenges would be to convince weary parents and guardians who would be suspect of colleges and "idealistic" career aspirations. The PRP and the educational pipeline engagement with Wagner needed to augment the academic and civic engagement components with concrete information and support regarding college access, realistic qualifications, knowledge, and strategies for gaining financial assistance. The results were to invite not only all high school freshmen to visit Wagner College and meet with a range of admission and financial administrators but also to encourage middle schoolers and their families to visit the campus. Along with the respective leadership and academic academies in each of the pipeline schools, campus interactions lowered local anxieties about building hopes for the youngsters. Nick created many such opportunities and interactions for parents and community members.

Another community benefit was the interaction among middle school, high school, and college students. The goal was to create effective pathways through the educational partnership. Enhanced reading programs were created for high school students in the PRHS Wagner/Raider Center and the reading alliance program for middle school students. The programs addressed not only educational skills but also many fears, apprehensions, and anxieties as part of the social and emotional growth of the middle and high school students. One clear goal and genuine benefit was to ease the orientation of twelve- and thirteen-year-old middle school graduates finding themselves in the presence of seventeen- and eighteen-year-old high schoolers. That age gap is dramatic physically, emotionally, and educationally. Pre-orientation through the pipeline practices eased the transition and likely increased the probabilities of successful high school performance.

At P.S. 21, Anthony Cosentino has set high standards for excellence in math, technology, and critical thinking. These are rarely the expectations that are set for public schools located in poor and working-class communities. Anthony is convinced that children will rise to the levels expected of them if they are encouraged and supported. All too often, schools in these districts feel overwhelmed with social, economic, and psychological pathologies, and higher expectations are unrealistic and quickly extinguished. To overcome this, schools must teach students to see beyond the social expectations placed upon them. Anthony frames his relationship with the children in his school around the question: What do you want to be and how can you get there? Anthony refuses to let the students be prisoners of what he terms the "truncated dreams" placed upon this neighborhood. He wants them to supersede the limits imposed on them socially by race, ethnicity, gender, home life, violence, and all the other barriers to learning what may be awaiting them. Toward this end, Anthony understood, like Nick, Andrew, and Tim, that the community needed to expand its vision of itself. To him, one of the critical benefits of the PRP is the inspiration it offered to the principals themselves. Collaborating with Wagner and its full cohort of students, faculty, and staff provided them with additional assets to encourage many parents and guardians to take the risk in believing that college readiness was an important pathway for the personal success of their children. It was not a pipe dream.

Andrew started by conducting a comprehensive program of empathy interviews, which demonstrated school leadership by first listening to the children, teachers, and the community. The goal was, and remains, helping each of these stakeholder groups to discover the leadership within themselves. It is about developing a purposeful sense of agency in those who often are ignored. To Anthony, this is the method to building the next generation of leaders who will insist on a more inclusive, just, and dynamic society. In this shadow neighborhood, here is a principal and teaching staff relying on all the benefits of college mentoring, tutoring, and college access for K–5 students. They learned to design digital portfolios. They discuss career possibilities with the students early in the process. Andrew exposes them to new experiences and possibilities from outside their neighborhood. At base, he believes that you can increase the happiness in children by tapping into their passions and interests through a pedagogy framed around compassion and empathy.

Andrew told me the partnership created the conditions to bring the school leaders together and trust each other rather than work in the usual building silos that are all too regular in large school systems. Their partners at Wagner College supported their creativity. They grew in confidence from the national conversation that they joined when presenting their work at higher education conferences, notably at the Coalition of Urban and Metropolitan Universities. Encouraged, they wrote more grants and increased their resources.

In the end, Anthony points to very clear data regarding student academic performance since the advent of the PRP pipeline. In the 2014–2015 academic year, only 9 percent of his third graders were at the passing rate on statewide language arts testing. In 2018–2019, the passing rate for third graders improved to 57.5 percent. The three principals are change agents in a community largely ignored and feared or invisible to the larger borough and school system. The PRP brought them together and they are changing destinies.

Nonprofit Community Partners: Dan Messina, CEO, Richmond University Medical Center; Susan Lamberti, Chair, Northfield Bank Foundation; Cesar Claro, President and CEO of the Staten Island Economic Development Corporation

For anchor partnerships to be successful, the participation of the key leaders and organizations in the community need to be engaged, supportive, and committed to the goals of the partnership. On Staten Island, the PRP had more than twenty such partners. The three I will mention are illustrative of how the community perceived the benefits derived from the partnership. Each played a significant role, as did a number of other participants.

Richmond University Medical Center (RUMC) is one of the two hospitals located on Staten Island. This capacity is remarkably low for a New York City borough that is larger in population than any large cities in the United States. RUMC resides in the heart of Port Richmond. Previously, it was St. Vincent's Hospital, run by the Sisters of Charity, and was part of the former famous St. Vincent's Hospital in the Greenwich Village neighborhood of Manhattan. It faced bankruptcy and reemerged as RUMC under new management. It serves the entire island but is the central health provider for the North Shore of Staten Island and the Port Richmond community in particular.

Under the leadership of its excellent CEO, Dan Messina, RUMC joined the PRP. Dan's personal life experiences and family history led him to become a leader in confronting multiple sclerosis. His mother suffered from this disease when he was growing up. He became a caregiver, which led to a career in public health, and later in health-care leadership. In line with these core values, Dan became a significant member of the PRP.

Beyond listing the benefits cited in the other profiles in this chapter, Dan noted other important impacts. Most importantly, the PRP helped the hospital in reestablishing its professional standing in the community. Underfunded, it is now finding its way to a more secure financial status. It has made significant gains from new legitimacy garnered from the support of the other partners. Most significant to Dan was the educational partnership with the Wagner College Evelyn Lindfors Spiro School of Nursing, a nationally ranked and highly regarded nursing program within the New York metropolitan area. In addition, the Wagner College Physician Assistant (PA) Program is highly ranked nationally. The most prestigious hospitals in New York City eagerly seek out the nursing school and PA program graduates. PRP benefits to RUMC were access to and employment of a significant number of these students. Many did clinical work and research with RUMC in responding to the health disparities evident in the Port Richmond neighborhood. These Wagner graduates are premium new professionals who are in high demand. RUMC now is able to attract a number of them to its staff.

Susan Lamberti spent her entire career in special education and disabilities. She was a local pioneer in this work when children with special needs were shunted or ignored. She retired from her teaching career in 2001. She raised a marvelous family, and her husband, Ralph, was a successful community leader, ultimately serving as borough president of Staten Island in the 1980s and later as a philanthropic leader. Soon after retirement, Susan was asked to volunteer as an expert for a novel program established by several local Rotary Club chapters in assisting victims of the civil war and ethnic genocide in the African nation of Sierra Leone. Children witnessed the murder and execution of their parents and siblings. Many barely escaped with their own lives after being mutilated by the roving gangs who amputated their legs or arms. The unspeakable nature of these horrors affected the hearts of the Rotary Clubs on Staten Island and they reached out to the hospitals to provide the amputees with needed surgeries for prosthetic limbs.

The hospitals would provide the surgery and convalescence pro bono and the Rotary Clubs would find neighbors to provide private homes for the children for six months or more. Susan volunteered for the program. Soon after, I was approached, along with our nursing school, to provide some needed recreational space and activity to support the children during this period. From that moment forward, I knew that Susan was laser-focused on the care and nurture of her community.

Years later, Susan joined the board of directors of one of the key banks on Staten Island, Northfield Savings. When the bank went public with its initial stock offering, it created its own local foundation with some of the profits from its initial stock sale in 2008. Susan became the chair of the board of the Northfield Savings Foundation. Along with the Richmond County Savings Foundation and the Staten Island Foundation, Northfield Savings became one of the key local funders of the PRP. The foundations' belief in the PRP proved crucial in support programs and personnel needed to implement a number of the partnership's key initiatives.

When I interviewed Susan about the benefits of the partnership, she was quite proud of the foundation's ability to fund the college access programs. Wagner reached out to the other two higher educational institutions on Staten Island, the College of Staten Island, part of CUNY, and the St. John's University campus on the island. Together we formed a coalition for college readiness and access in two other neighborhoods of need in a program we called 30,000 Degrees. Through the work of the coalition, we hoped to increase the number of two- and four-year degrees on Staten Island by that additional number in ten years. The bank foundations led that funding effort. Susan and the others believed that the initiative was necessary for the health and welfare of the entire borough. She sees the pipeline model of the PRP as an essential benefit to this community and as a consequence to the entire economy of the island. Susan understands that networking the schools brings economic benefits to the entire borough.

Cesar Claro serves in two important public leadership roles. He is the executive director of the Richmond County Savings Foundation and serves as the president and CEO of the Staten Island Economic Development Corporation (SIEDC), the leading force in attracting and sustaining business and economic growth in the borough. Its members represent all the major business, banking, health care, higher education, finance, and development entities that constitute much of Staten Island's economy and employment. Economic growth on the island had been quite significant until the COVID-19 pandemic. To continue this trajectory, the SIEDC leadership understood the ever-increasing need for a more educated and technologically skilled workforce.

When I interviewed Cesar for this book, he cited the benefits of having a greater number of college degrees in the community. Staten Island currently trails Brooklyn, Manhattan, and Queens in the number of adults with two- or four-year degrees. Only the Bronx ranks below Staten Island. "Any time a major college gets involved in community development, particularly in partnerships with local high schools, it's going to be a success," Cesar told me. "The Port Richmond Partnership and the 30,000 Degrees program were no exception. The teaching and mentoring components were crucial and the emphasis on telling young people about the importance of getting a college education was the difference maker. As a founder, I'd say that we love these types of partnerships." He went on to stress the value added of creating genuine college access to students from neighborhoods that have little experience with colleges. The parents often fear getting beyond their means, hesitant to elevate their children's aspirations for something that is reserved for populations that are economically privileged. The need to break through these barriers is a necessary goal for the continued economic progress of the borough.

The partnership always presented itself to the business community and the island's elected leaders as a nonpartisan civic initiative. It represented people and neighborhoods as part of the larger social fabric of the borough. This approach kept the focus on the community, the children, and the parents and away from the ever-present cultural stereotypes lingering around the edges of the public narrative of legitimacy and formal citizenship. The impact provided solid reasons for the funders and various elected officials to support the partnership. As Cesar explained his local leadership role and how it fit this work, "I am most proud of putting Staten Island on the map by hosting significant events, securing important grants, and organizing the business community." He sees the PRP benefits as clearly in line with these objectives.

Arlette Cepeda: Parent, Artist, Community Partner, PRP Leader

Arlette Cepeda's life and her contributions to civic engagement present themselves as a composite profile of the different constituencies benefiting from anchor partnerships. Her observations about the benefits to the community derive from the different identities that she has experienced as a neighborhood resident, parent of children in the PRP educational pipeline, local artist, campus civic engagement leader, and now a key leader of one of the PRP's nonprofit community partners. Her perspective is unique and comprehensive.

Arlette was born in the Bronx, but her family returned to its homeland in the Dominican Republic where she completed her education through high school. As a child, she loved the arts, particularly ballet, the violin, and fine arts. She returned to the United States for college, studying art at Parsons School of Design, and then graduated from the more affordable Hunter College/CUNY. She married, had two children, and struggled to sustain a decent standard of living for her family. Unfortunately, the marriage dissolved and she took her children back to the Dominican Republic. She found a new life with another visual artist and had a third child. Once more, she returned, with all of them in tow, to New York City where she found interesting work as a teaching artist for *The New York Times* Visions Program and later, for several years, with the Alvin Ailey Dance Company's youth programs. She continued with her own artwork. In short, Arlette faced economic challenges throughout her life, so she was no stranger to the everyday lives of shadow neighborhoods.

Based on her friendship with a local media artist who also worked for Wagner College's Communications Department, Arlette applied for the position of coordinator of Wagner's Center for Leadership and Community Engagement (CLCE), the hub of its civic engagement programs. Her responsibilities revolved around cultivating and nurturing the college's relationships with its PRP community partners. As Arlette was providing invaluable contributions to the center and the PRP, she was learning more about the educational and intellectual foundations of democratic education. This was a new field for her. She was also growing as a campus administrator. Her life in Port Richmond allowed her to bring a fresh perspective to her Wagner colleagues and our community partners. She proved herself under the brilliant mentoring of our director, Samantha Siegel, herself a young force of nature in civic work. Once we had an opening, Arlette eventually became the CLCE director. She oversaw our Bonner Scholars Program, civically engaged faculty and students and the PRP Board of Directors, and managed budgets, grants, and donor stewardship. For most of this time, she reported directly to the President's Office. In short, she was at the center of all of the work inside the campus and throughout the community.

When I interviewed Arlette for this book, she had left Wagner to become deputy director of La Colmena, a worker cooperative for Port Richmond immigrants that is an active community partner in the PRP. In preparation for our conversation, Arlette carefully organized her thoughts. She identified five specific benefits and stakeholder groups. She listed the pipeline students as the primary recipients. As she put it, they are "distanced by otherness by a society that sends clear messages that they exist outside of the social core. They need to overcome this sense of social estrangement." To Arlette, the pipeline's students are exposed to the Bonner Scholars and other civically engaged students at Wagner who serve as their elder mentors, role models, and activists. The pipeline students are moved in ways that inspire a sense that they can aspire to a vocation and are shown pathways for a career starting as early as the elementary years at P.S. 21. In their high school years, they are asked to become interns and activists in their own civic work as part of the PRPLA. Arlette offered several examples, including Sebastian, a PRHS student who was running the food pantry program at one of the partner organizations in his junior year.

Arlette identified the benefits to the community derived from civically engaged faculty research that addressed local needs and issues. She cited the research of Professor Margarita Sanchez who focused on the separate and little understood language of Mixteco, which was indigenous to the Oaxacan people in San Jeronimo, Mexico, the homeland of many Port Richmond immigrants. The faculty learned to treat the Oaxacan community with respect and promise. Staff at the partner organizations and on campus were touched by the growth they witnessed in the pipeline students. This advanced the respective staff's sense of purpose in their own work.

Arlette spoke about the benefits the organizational partners gained. They were able to expand the reach and impact of their community service by gaining so many extra resources and voluntary labor. Arlette cited studies that the PRP advanced through connecting other universities. One of many examples was the collaboration with the Massachusetts Institute of Technology on a study of the contributions of undocumented workers to the Staten Island economy. Another involved a study of the Staten Island waterfront after the impact of Hurricane Sandy. She stated that the community partner organizations gained more knowledge of their own community. This increased their effectiveness and their abilities to seek more grant and governmental funding.

Finally, Arlette spoke to the overall benefit to the Port Richmond community. All areas of the community's well-being were advanced, from its economic, educational, and leadership capacity to its social identity, which was most dramatically advanced by the PRP projects in the fine and performing arts. The community took notice of the public arts and exhibitions that illustrated its assets, challenges, and aspirations. The arts elevated the community's self-esteem and identity.

Summary

This chapter presented the quantifiable and qualitative impacts of anchor partnerships. From the previous chapters, we can see the rich effect of civic engagement on the learning and lives of students, staff, and faculty members as well as the campus culture. In this chapter, we can better understand how partnerships directly benefit the community, the partner organizations, and the local economy. Both sides of the partnerships illustrate the rich experiences benefiting individuals, participating institutions, and overall community prosperity. To be successful, the partnerships entail a great deal of work and excellent leadership across the board. In the end, it is transformational work that changes lives in real and palpable ways. For the larger society, American democracy gains knowledgeable, informed, and committed citizens. The ripple effect of this effort is essential in the midst of a social epoch marked by racial, economic, and political divisions challenging the very viability of democracy itself.

Notes

1. See "Our History" at www.democracycollaborative.org.

2. See University of Pennsylvania: FY 2020 Economic and Social Impact Report, http://www.evp.upenn.edu/pdf/FY-20-economic-and-social-impact.pdf.

3. See "Step by Step Economic Anchor Inclusion," Drexel University, https://drexel.edu/civicengagement/centers-initiatives/economic-inclusion/step-by-step, 2020.

4. See "Hopkins Local Three-Year Progress Report," Hub, Johns Hopkins University, https://hub.jhu.edu/2019/02/20/hopkinslocal-year-three-progress-report/, 2020.

5. See *Lenfest North Philadelphia Workforce Initiative Annual Report, 2019–20*, Temple University, https://templelnpwi.org/wp-content/uploads/2021/01/fy-19-20-annual-impact-report-final-draft.pdf.

6. See "The Third Ward Initiative: Moving Forward," March 24, 2021, https://uh.edu/third-Ward.

7. See "Ogden Can," https://www.weber.edu/ogdencan/partners.html.

8. See Ralph Ellison, prologue to *Invisible Man*, 2nd ed. (New York: Vintage Books, 1980), 14.

9

THE ROLE OF THE NATIONAL ASSOCIATIONS OF HIGHER EDUCATION

With the expansion of the civic mission across a large number of colleges and universities, the national higher education associations have prioritized civic engagement and democratic citizenship. These associations provide important resources and leadership in support of community-based learning and the anchor institution approach. Most importantly, their practices have developed over the past decade by integrating their civic programs with their commitments to increasing ethnic diversity, equity, and inclusion. This proves to be a significant shift. While diversity programs maintain a relatively autonomous space supporting the indictment of the long history of racial and ethnic subordination and provide essential arenas for people of color to gather, connect, and support one another, the commitment to a participatory and interracial democracy is a cherished and shared goal of the civic and antiracist agendas, respectively. There is no just democracy without a fundamental allegiance to full social inclusion, economic equity, and engaged citizenship.

The anchor approach joins universities with shadow neighborhoods. As such, I believe it promises the most advanced work in combining the democratic civic project with the ideals of greater diversity, equity, and inclusion. Fundamentally, anchor partnerships position universities to be central partners in addressing the nation's commitment to political, economic, and social transformation. This returns higher education to its historic civic mission, namely, preparing learners to be informed and engaged citizens who are committed to a free and dynamic nation. It reissues Benjamin Franklin's vision for a higher education system that prizes a practical and broad education, both serving as essential ingredients in forging economic prosperity and political freedom. While these ideals originally were born amid the severe contradictions of slavery, female subordination, and class inequality, they nonetheless provide a framework for democratic aspirations and the appropriate engagement and transformation of our current failures.

For these partnerships to be successful, some necessary principles must be satisfied. As I have argued earlier in this book, first and foremost, the relationship between the university and the neighborhood must be reciprocal. There needs to be interpersonal affinity, institutional respect, shared resources, engaged leadership, and mutual gain. All of these constitute a reciprocal relationship. The university benefits from increased student learning outcomes and retention, greater student civic competency, strategic applied research, faculty engagement, enhanced philanthropy, and especially the cultivation and successful development of future generations of college students who otherwise would not have been available to them. Neighborhoods gain access to social and physical capital, expertise, college awareness and readiness, enhanced resources in health services and related social areas, and, most importantly, increased interest and engagement of residents within their own communities. The neighborhood's self-esteem grows and the university's civic practice increases campus pride.

Successful partnerships must be fiscally and politically sustainable. I made the case for fiscal benefits in chapter 5. The question of leadership is one I will take up in the last chapter, but the cultivation and support for civically engaged institutional leadership falls within the mission of the national higher education and the national civic associations. Each of them plays a unique role in advancing the anchor work. They offer educational, professional, and financial support for institutional leaders and faculty members. The national higher educational associations are, themselves, anchor institutions for universities and colleges. They are varied in their missions, constituencies, and practices. What follows is a brief overview of the major associations connected to the civic renewal project for higher education.

Anchor Institutions Task Force

Founded in 2009, the Anchor Institutions Task Force (AITF) is an individual membership network that focuses on the advancement of anchor practice. It registers more than 900 individual members and holds an annual two-day meeting. While initially beginning with a single focus on higher education anchor institutions, AITF is now a cross-disciplinary association. It is more reflective of the neighborhood anchor partnerships that reach across higher education, K–12 schools, hospitals and health-care organizations, and economic development. The network produces a number of publications and policy papers. Active subgroups within AITF meet separately as well as at the annual meeting. AITF's major leaders are Ira Harkavy, Nancy Cantor, and its chief executive officer, David Maurrasse. The work of the organization flows through Marga Inc., David's consulting group.

AITF was founded in the winter of 2008–2009. A group of the association's founders were advising the U.S. Department of Housing and Urban Development (HUD) on how it could benefit from advancing university anchor partnerships. Shortly afterward, the AITF network was launched. At that time, AITF's major focus was on large universities with important schools of education, medicine, and nursing, because these units maintained a significant physical, service, and policy presence in economically challenged neighborhoods.

As we have discussed earlier, AITF maintains core values in promoting place-based reciprocal and democratic partnerships and by emphasizing the fundamental importance of addressing issues and challenges of equity and social justice in its practice. In the decade following AITF's founding, word spread about the compelling nature of the anchor concept. It flowed throughout the civic engagement community within higher education and then into the aligned areas of health and hospitals, neighborhood and local economic development, and then to urban policymakers and local government officials. As a result of some important relationships, the international educational community showed interest in the anchor concept. An international consortium emerged, typically hosting biannual meetings in Europe under the organizing guidance of the Council of Europe's Higher Education Commission.

AITF is not a philanthropy or a foundation. It does not distribute grants to its members; rather, it provides them with a forum for ideas, shared practice, innovative approaches to anchor challenges, and, in particular, a growing network for anchor practitioners. It takes a nonpartisan approach with a deep commitment to its core values, namely the pursuit of equity, social justice, and democratic practice, and the importance of place. It focuses on policy and practice, not on ideology or the established political entities. It is branching into the public sphere and, consequently, local elected officials have found common ground with anchor institutions in fostering collaborative efforts to address economic inequality and its attendant consequences in local schooling, health care, and economic development.

As an arena for addressing best practices, AITF is becoming an influential space for advancing both domestic and international anchor partnerships and anchor work. It now has an online journal and various webinars. I have watched the insightful work produced by both the health professional subgroup and the economic professionals subgroup. They are authoring promising approaches that align the practice and resources of their respective institutional partners. As a young organization, AITF has established itself as an important arena for the advancement of anchor partnerships. It maintains significant potential for becoming the national voice of the value of anchor partnerships to local and federal agencies as well as government leaders and legislators.

The impact of the COVID-19 worldwide pandemic on shadow neighborhoods is pervasive and debilitating. It has exposed and extended the acute social disparities in health and the de facto educational apartheid that are endemic in Brown and Black communities. David Maurrasse is convinced that anchor institutions must play an even larger role in addressing these issues. He recently told me that AITF and anchor partners must engage as never before. He envisions an increased AITF emphasis on policy as well as practice. This inevitably will require a role for AITF in advocating for the renewal of HUD's Community Outreach Partnership Centers (COPC) and a dramatic increase in funding for local anchor partnerships.

The Association of American Colleges and Universities

As the largest association advocating for undergraduate and liberal education, the Association of American Colleges and Universities (AAC&U) is composed of approximately 1,500 university and college institutional members. Founded in 1915, the association's main mission is the strengthening of liberal learning, which is not to be confused with liberal politics. AAC&U promotes independent and critical thinking, effective communication skills, social responsibility, civic competency, and a full commitment to diversity, equity, and inclusion. It has served as a highly impactful intellectual reservoir for pedagogical and educational reform for thousands of university administrators, faculty members, and institutional leaders.

Carol Geary Schneider, PhD, served as its transformational leader from 1998 to 2016. Her tenure at AAC&U marked a dramatic turning point in the substance and size of the organization. She focused on reconnecting traditional liberal education with its central civic purposes. Through a number of well-funded national programs, she led AAC&U in engaging its core constituency with the most substantive literature and innovative scholarship around race, gender, and democracy. Employing learning community pedagogy in dispersing resources, AAC&U invited hundreds of campuses into dialogues around the meaning, purpose, and impact of higher education in a modern pluralist and diverse society.

AAC&U sponsored numerous campus programs, hosted intensive and meaningful annual and regional conferences, and provided cutting-edge research and publications to assist campuses in providing generations of students with the knowledge, intellectual skills, and social skills for a diverse, inclusive, and just democratic society. In the late 1980s and early 1990s, AAC&U received a generous grant from the National Endowment for the Humanities toward these goals. From that came a national initiative titled Engaging Cultural Legacies: Shaping Core Curricula in the Humanities. The central aim was to help college faculty and leaders on sixty-three campuses encounter both the traditional and new historical, literary, and social science scholarship around the plurality of cultures both domestically and internationally. In essence this became a national learning community across the campuses of the participants and then within their respective communities. It proved to be another form of graduate education for many already seasoned scholars and faculty members. The project provided an encounter with the rich literature that broadened the historical and social fabric of the humanities and social sciences.

The culture war over the American college curriculum that began in the 1980s with Alan Bloom's influential book, *The Closing of the American Mind*, intensified during the Clinton decade. This included mounting resistance to providing greater access to a college education to those previously omitted, namely, Black, Brown, and Asian students, as well as greater numbers of women. Opponents cast the access as diluting the meaning of a degree and abandoning the importance of meritocracy. Under the banner of multiculturalism, adversaries perceived great campus diversity as diluting their core principle that "merit" was the singular arbiter of value. At that moment, Schneider led AAC&U to join the concepts of diversity and democracy. Instead of presenting greater diversity within the curriculum and campus population as "set asides" for previously exploited ethnic, racial, and gender populations, she bravely and correctly reestablished the inherent relationship between American pluralism and American democracy.

From this new perspective, AAC&U launched another critical national program, American Commitments, where the founding documents of the American republic were joined with the best old and new scholarship regarding the civic mission for a pluralist democracy. Again the national learning community method supported this work on many campuses, both directly through grants and indirectly through conferences, dialogues, and scholarship.

AAC&U's growing focus on diversity, democracy, and justice provided an important pedagogical and intellectual home for college leaders and college civic practitioners. Having served on its board of directors twice and having chaired the board once, I had an intimate understanding of the evolution of the conjunction of what emerged initially as relatively autonomous realms of diversity work and, separately, civic engagement, particularly community-based learning. A major advancement was underway within AAC&U with the seminal publication of *A Crucible Moment: College Learning and Democracy's Future,* developed by the National Task Force on Civic Learning and Democratic Engagement in 2012. Under the brilliant facilitation and primary authorship of Caryn McTighe Musil, this important work was presented at a major White House conference and widely distributed to all member campuses and well beyond. The civic work of the organization ascended in importance to the overall renewal of undergraduate learning and liberal education. Colleges were urged to again prize their historic mission of educating and preparing students as engaged citizens for a robust democracy.

Most recently, President Lynn Pasquerella has led AAC&U in increasing its commitments to diversity, equity, and inclusion through its new national program, Truth, Racial Healing & Transformation (TRHT). With generous external funding, AAC&U is working with cohorts of campuses participating in substantive and challenging work in recognizing and engaging the long history of America's racial bigotry and violence while seeking methods and solutions in assisting campuses to become centers for their stakeholders and local communities. This work brings AAC&U closer to the anchor partnership work.

Each of these national associations plays a unique role in support of the democratic renewal project. The AITF is directly engaged in anchor partnerships. AAC&U predominantly concentrates on the education of undergraduates. It overlaps with the anchor mission, but its connection to neighborhood transformation is less direct. AAC&U's affinity to the anchor project runs through the universal provision of a broad, deep, and substantive education for the vast majority of society. In that work, AAC&U is about expanding access and support for all students in building an antiracist educational foundation for generations of citizens. While its programs are not directly about neighborhood educational pipelines and political transformation, the organization is at the center of the intellectual, developmental, and moral underpinnings of anchor work. In this sense, it is a major partner.

The Coalition of Urban and Metropolitan Universities

Founded in the 1989 by university leaders, the Coalition for Urban and Metropolitan Universities (CUMU) focuses on the university's role as a steward of place. An earlier chapter featured some of the organization's history. Currently, CUMU maintains approximately ninety institutional members, with the large majority engaged in some form of anchor work with their local communities. This is a network known for its strategic focus on higher education's important role in the metropolitan and urban space. Given their locations, these institutions are immersed in issues of diversity, opportunity, and local impact. The limited size of the coalition allows for intimate dialogues about shared practice in engaging the urban economic, social, and educational environment.

CUMU's executive director is Bobbie Laur. Like Carol Schneider's impact on AAC&U, Bobbie's brilliant, resilient, and insightful leadership tripled the coalition's membership and diversified its geographic footprint and institutional type. Having had the privilege of serving and chairing the organization's board of directors, I can personally testify to the generative cross-institutional relationships emerging within CUMU. It is fast becoming an important arena for institutional leaders in thinking strategically about the unique challenges facing cities and suburbs and the imperative of engaged universities assisting in finding sustainable solutions to what can seem at times to be immutable barriers to progress.

Anchor partnerships are a major priority within CUMU. Recently, the coalition partnered with The Democracy Collaborative (TDC), an international research and development lab for democratizing the economy. Together they formed the Anchor Learning Network. Initially, thirty-one colleges and universities joined in this effort to expand their institutional roles in deploying their assets in advancing civic and economic prosperity in their local communities. This new initiative will sharpen the anchor practice of CUMU colleges and universities by focusing on the material and educational impact of their civic and anchor work. Some of this effort includes the alignment of university spending and hiring practices with local employment and economic needs.

Through the use of civic metrics, CUMU members will focus more directly on addressing the coefficients of the inequality that is endemic in their urban and metropolitan settings. This type of anchor work will grow the depth and breadth of the neighborhood partnerships as it shares best practices and the most promising assessment tools in promoting the local economy and small business partners, forging greater local health-care access and services, building educational pipelines, and expanding neighborhood and institutional leadership within diverse neighborhoods. CUMU is now an important arena for those institutions and their leaders who are committed to the anchor model.

Campus Compact

Campus Compact is the largest national civic engagement organization, with approximately one thousand institutional members. More than four hundred and fifty university and college presidents signed Compact's thirtieth-anniversary action statement. While the COVID-19 pandemic will have an impact on the membership list of all national organizations in higher education, Compact's civic footprint will remain impressive. It holds the promise of sustained national student engagement with the enduring inequalities that are paramount in shadow communities, particularly within the pre-K–12 school system.

Several university presidents and national leaders founded Compact in the mid-1980s to increase student concern for the public good, especially by an enhanced commitment to voting and civic responsibility. The organization ushered in service learning in the 1990s, and then it embraced a larger institutional civic engagement mission that encompassed the entire campus community. As civic renewal spread, Campus Compact eventually moved closer to an anchor institution orientation with its formalization of an action statement in 2016. Having chaired the Compact board of directors at that time, I have a thorough understanding of the significance of that moment for the strategic direction of the organization. Compact's transformative president, Andrew Seligsohn, led this major advance.

Presidents committed to a broad declaration that has a more far-reaching effect than the Compact's original agreement or its 1999 President's Declaration on Civic Responsibility. The 2016 statement responded to the growing public polarization and the acute increase in economic inequality. Most notably, it called for "empowering students, faculty, staff, and community partners to create mutually respectful partnerships in pursuit of a just, equitable, and sustainable future for communities beyond the campus."[1] Further, the statement required signatories to establish civic action plans for their respective campuses within one year.

In the eighteen months that followed, approximately 200 colleges and universities were engaged in the process of presenting civic action plans and 120 had fully developed them. Most of these consisted of some form of anchor partnerships. Each one responded to the local challenges in its partner community. Inevitably, these plans included issues of local inequality. Many of these partnerships contain specific collaborations with their respective K–12 schools and health-care systems. As these planning processes matured, Campus Compact's national office moved into a more defined understanding, and ultimately a greater commitment to issues of diversity, equity, and inclusion as an essential element of civic engagement. The national office role included providing materials, facilitation models, and analytics for inclusive support of anchor work.

The democratic vision of Campus Compact currently encompasses a "full participation" approach to its civic practice. In its new Compact 20 mission, the organization intensified its priority to involving student voices and ideas into its on-the-ground work in schools, health care, economic development, and the environment. Compact 20 is about providing professional development and networking opportunities for community partners, community engagement professionals, faculty members, and university leaders. These services range from direct training in all aspects of civic engagement work, syllabi and educational resources for faculty members, an accessible online library, voter education and registration programs, and leadership development. Compact offers toolkits for directing research in support of solutions to local, national, and global issues. It presents both a significant body of useful publications and opportunities for engaged faculty research on civic work. Moreover, it focuses on the development of student civic competencies, establishing pathways for students to connect with one another through a program of fellowships around democratic and equity initiatives.

Campus Compact continues many forums for networking through a biannual national conference and many local dialogues, conferences, and gatherings. It provides an impressive arena for civic work. In recent years it has expanded the number of community colleges within the network of institutions. It welcomed The Democracy Commitment (TDC) into its ranks, although it has proven to be a somewhat more complicated merger than once believed. While TDC's membership includes 221 community colleges, the degrees of actual collaboration are best measured at the local level. This is an emerging part of Compact's strategy, and TDC has been renamed Community Colleges for Democracy. This full merger is under development, and in the future TDC could emerge on its own once again.

Ultimately, Campus Compact believes in the development of a new generation of students, campus stakeholders, and community partners as agents of change in pursuit of healthy communities. Higher education's civic renewal will need a vibrant, active, and successful Campus Compact.

The Bonner Leaders Program of the Bonner Foundation

In 1990, the Bonner Foundation initiated a scholarship program to assist students in completing college through a community service-framed model. The organization's founding director, Wayne Meisel, had an impressive history in the civic engagement world as the founder of the Campus Outreach Opportunity League (COOL), an organization mobilizing college students to strengthen communities through service and action. Wayne deployed a similar model with the Bonner Foundation. Through various initiatives over the next thirty years, the foundation built an impressive network of participating colleges that would provide scholarship funds in support of economically challenged students through a four-year program of leadership, service, and reflection. Ultimately, the Bonner Leaders Program matured into one of the most effective efforts in joining civic engagement, academic learning, and social and emotional growth with preparation for democratic citizenship and civic professionalism.

Bobby Hackett now serves as Bonner's president after years of leading its work in student development and civic action. He is another remarkable teacher and mentor for anchor and civic work. I can personally testify to the efficacy of the Bonner model. Many of the students I introduced in earlier chapters owe a great deal of their civic competency to Bonner's leadership development program. The program excels at civic leadership through an intentional four-year educational landscape of direct client service, education and reflection, capacity building and social action, and action research. It is a rich curriculum that combines experiential and civic engagement (300 hours per academic year) with the best skills of liberal learning.

Through the four undergraduate years, students complete appropriate capstones for each of these educational goals. The program possesses an elegant scaffolding of concepts, experiences, and reflection. I previously introduced you to Anthony Tucker Bartley, who went through the Bonner Leaders Program at Wagner College and who is now finishing his medical degree at Harvard University Medical School. His story is a perfect example of the Bonner model. He was raised with love and care by his mother. As an African American young man, he was keenly aware of what the lack of equity does to poor and struggling communities. As Anthony moved through the stages of the program, he gained confidence, skill, and expertise. He is dedicated to medicine, and his intention is to serve shadow communities of need. His Wagner and Bonner experiences helped him discover his calling and prepared him to become an emerging leader in community medicine.

The importance of the Bonner Leaders Program for anchor work is that it provides an important educational structure for students' personal development as well as their achievement of civic competency. Bonner has approximately sixty-five member campuses. Others have shown great interest in applying for network membership. While membership does require some commitment to greater scholarship funds for Bonner students, it usually is not a barrier to entry. In Bonner's strategic plan, the board has set a goal of 20 percent of graduating students for every member institution. Institutions that are not likely to join the Bonner Leaders Program would be wise to adopt its leadership model, because the Bonner method provides a pedagogy of practice that has proven to be highly effective.

The American Democracy Project of the American Association of State Colleges and Universities

The American Democracy Project (ADP), formed in 2003 by the American Association of State Colleges and Universities (AASCU) in partnership with *The New York Times*, serves as a network of almost 300 public colleges and universities that work toward greater student civic knowledge and civic engagement in preparation for democratic leadership. ADP is a nonpartisan effort in citizenship education. By acquiring the appropriate skills, habits, knowledge, and civic engagement, participating students learn "the arts of democracy." The network provides an arena to promote and support multi-campus and individual campus projects that range across any number of disciplines.

ADP is an earlier project that was part of the civic renewal in higher education. It is more indicative of the advancement of service learning and campus civic engagement at the turn of the century. It predates the evolution to the anchor partnership concept, but it has adapted to support that work. Like its parent organization, AASCU, this network is an important portal for civic work within the state college sector. It assists the chancellors, presidents, and senior leadership of these institutions in presenting and promoting the importance and granular impact of this work on students and local communities. As stewards of place, AASCU schools see their public role as inherently anchored within their local communities, where a significant share of their students and campus stakeholders reside.

Through publications, community-based research and teaching, annual and local conferences, community dialogues, and other formats, ADP assists in supporting the civic commitments of state colleges and universities. In many ways, ADP is an important clearinghouse for best practices and shared learning among its member institutions.

The Democracy Commitment

As mentioned earlier, The Democracy Commitment (TDC) was founded by a number of public community colleges with the aim of establishing their specific role in advancing civic engagement and citizenship education. When TDC formed, it found an administrative home within AASCU and ADP. It since went on its own and eventually aligned with Campus Compact. As the fastest growing sector of higher education, and in many ways the most diverse by class, race, and ethnicity, community colleges must play a major role in the civic renewal of higher education as well as a prime leadership position within anchor partnerships.

One of the sector's major leaders is Brian Murphy, who was president of De Anza College, near San Jose, California. Brian has an enduring commitment to bring civic practice into the mainstream of community college life. Too often, community colleges are understood as narrow, skill-based educational institutions that are preparing students exclusively for specific jobs and careers. TDC consists of more than two hundred and fifty community colleges that prioritize career specialization as part of a broader education that also prepares students to be engaged citizens. As such, its potential for an important role in anchor partnerships remains critical if anchor university-neighborhood partnerships are to be successful in addressing the deep inequalities within the American educational system. Economic and social inequality is the life lived within the corridors of these institutions.

Specialized Associations

Bringing Theory to Practice (BTtoP) describes itself as a community of educators working on issues of higher education innovation and social transformation. It originally specialized in connecting civic engagement, academic achievement, and reducing barriers to student learning. It focused on the social and emotional growth of students in their personal lives. The core belief underlying the work revolves around the power of civic engagement on personal self-esteem and, consequently, academic success, particularly for students struggling with any number of limiting personal choices. Don Harward, president emeritus of Bates College, was the founding director.

BTtoP has moved well beyond this original mission. It developed a more expansive vision of educational reform in relation to the larger inequalities inherent in the American social milieux. It has become a significant resource of modest grants to individual institutions that are engaged with issues of deep learning, particularly in the areas of diversity, equity, inclusion, and transformation. These small grants often underwrite innovative campus initiatives as they support and empower engaged faculty and staff reformers.

BTtoP links to anchor work through these myriad projects that almost always have civic practice embedded in the work. As such, it is an important arena available to campus clusters that require both resources and affirmation around transformative practice. The organization has funded hundreds of such efforts since 2003. David Scobey, a longtime scholar and active public intellectual, is the current director. Under his leadership, BTtoP will continue to drive its intellectual and place-centered foundation.

Imagining America (IA) was founded at the University of Michigan in 1999. The organization offers another unique position in the larger tapestry of higher education civic renewal and community empowerment. It operates as a consortium of educators in the humanities, the arts, digital media, and design. This is a space for the role of the cultural arts to inform, support, and expand its influence on community participation and the university as anchor institution.

The performing arts and public history often advance and fuel social change. They are able to feature the experience and texture of those communities that are ignored in the national narrative. Race, gender, ethnicity, and class issues inform much of this practice. The visual arts and digital media are such powerful arenas for learning, and IA emphasizes its use in institutional reform and community empowerment. It offers a larger variety of resources that are shared through conferences, an online journal, fellowships, dialogues, and more. Gatherings are remarkably uplifting events that combine performance and intellectual exchanges. This organization provides a key portal for anchor partners in the arts and humanities.

Project Pericles is a consortium of thirty member institutions, mostly liberal arts colleges, that was founded in the late 1990s by Eugene Lang, a noted and important philanthropist, to support democracy and justice. Its work primarily centers on educational pathways for civic learning and community engagement. It offers an important methodology of mapping all the different ways the university touches its local community and others it engages. While small in size, Pericles offers some influential practices that can be shared with nonmembers to support civically engaged faculty and staff members on many other campuses.

Going Forward: Building a National Anchor Impact

From the vantage point of the shadow communities and their partner campuses, these various national associations and networks provide opportunities in advancing the transformative and inclusive democratic project at the local level. The campus leaders uniquely have access to them. The key to local success resides in deploying the distinctive assets and platforms of the national organizations as they assist in enhancing the local partnership. Bringing campus participants as well as community partners to these national gatherings is quite significant. For the national organizations and the attending audiences, the local partnerships demonstrate the impact of their work on both the campus and the community while also presenting the challenges and barriers to continued success. Local partners who attend are able to view the emerging national constituency of the anchor partnerships. The affirmation afforded to the campus/community team is invaluable in building their self-esteem and political resiliency for the ever-present challenges that abound.

The imperative for the national organizations is twofold. First, these entities need to harvest and support the local practices. They must digest and ultimately provide a scholarship of civic and anchor practices. This is part of their larger educational and scholarly missions. Second, these respective national organizations must find ways to collaborate with one another in supporting the local work and building the national anchor brand. Collectively, the national organizations possess the potential to expand the impact of local democracy through anchor work. They nationalize the anchor approach to building local, inclusive, and transformative democratic entities through educating public officials, legislatures, educational policymakers, philanthropies, and other potential partners.

Of course, this type of national collaboration is quite difficult. The organizations I highlighted, as well as others unmentioned, serve specific memberships and constituencies. To a degree, they exist in a somewhat competitive educational universe. To overcome this type of inertia, AAC&U led the effort for greater shared work when it founded the CLDE network after the publication and White House launch of *A Crucible Moment* in 2012. CLDE meetings are attempts at greater coordination around all of the respective civic engagement priorities of the respective associations. While important, the full potential of CLDE remains a work in progress.

Campuses have additional potential allies in bringing university-neighborhood partnerships to national attention and having a greater impact: higher education accreditors. These regional organizations possess significant influence through the establishment and assessment of college and university values, goals, and priorities. All campuses that wish to participate in the federal educational loan programs must receive full accreditation from one of the five regionally established accreditors. For the very large majority of colleges and universities, exclusion from the federal loan program would virtually bankrupt them.

In turn, the accreditors reflect back to their respective university and college participants the values established in the founding missions and strategic plans of the individual campuses. The accrediting boards are representative of higher education much like the licensing boards in medicine, law, and accounting. These accreditation boards seek specific assessments of the civic work of the participating institutions. They have drawn from a number of best practices in establishing metrics for the role of civic engagement within undergraduate education. The Higher Learning Commission, the largest of the regional accreditors, established civic engagement as a core value in higher education assessment. Specifically, "the institution provides opportunities for civic engagement in a diverse multicultural society and globally connected world, as appropriate within its mission and the constituencies it serves."[2] The impact of these types of core standards can be immense for universities and colleges. For anchor campus/community partnerships, they provide a firm foundation in legitimizing and supporting the work. In sum, with the roles of the national higher education associations and their efforts to collaborate around the civic renewal agenda, the regional accreditation associations are providing a major opportunity for the normalization and growth of anchor partnerships.

In the next chapter, I will conclude by reviewing the current and future promise and challenges for these partnerships in light of the fiscal dilemmas confronting universities and colleges. Finally, I will look at the larger impact of these partnerships on a potentially new type of democratic politics.

Notes

1. See "Action Statement of Presidents and Chancellors," Campus Compact, www.compact.org.

2. Higher Education Learning Commission, "Criteria for Accreditation," 2019, https://hlcommission.org/policies/criteria-and-core-components.html.

10

TOWARD NEIGHBORHOOD DEMOCRACY AND THE ENGAGED UNIVERSITY

The argument of this book is that universities and poor, working-class communities are tied together in a symbiotic relationship. For each to rise above the economic crises that envelop them, they need to be anchors and allies for one another. These neighborhoods are drowning in a sea of economic, health, and educational disparities. While they possess certain cultural and social assets, they are in dire need of new allies who possess social as well as financial capital that will assist them in rising above the economic and educational systemic limits surrounding them. Meanwhile, universities are, themselves, in the midst of a cataclysmic moment fraught with fiscal, demographic, and technological challenges that are overwhelming. Colleges and shadow neighborhoods relying on the government to rescue them seems highly problematic on political and fiscal grounds. Both need to partner and create their own political and social alliance in advancing each other's progress.

For colleges and universities, their futures rest on at least three major factors. First, they must increase their enrollments in order to sustain themselves financially. In part this requires them to augment their current enrollment pools by identifying, preparing, and growing a new generation of college students from traditionally underserved populations. My argument throughout this book has demonstrated the anchor educational pipeline model as an effective strategy for student success for potential first-generation college populations.

Second, universities need to reorganize their business models. The current approach of tuition increases accompanied by escalating institutional financial aid—the "discount" model—is proving to be an unsustainable financial strategy for private and some public institutions. It has created a "financial bubble" much like the subprime mortgage bubble of the Great Recession in 2008. The consequence is that no one competitive institution has enough market presence to resist the centrifugal force of lowering the effective price. Like most "tragedies of the commons," all parties fail together. For the majority of public institutions, their business models have relied on state appropriations to supplement lower tuition and fees. With the decline in state appropriations, these institutions have been forced to increase tuition and fees. This is a failed strategy because the political pushback has been significant, while at the same time, students and families are sinking under a mountain of student debt. In the end, the delivery of education, the methods and locations of learning, and the productivity of the faculty and staff are all subject to significant change in order for higher education to lower the cost of educating students.

Finally, higher education must recover the public trust and belief in the net value of a college degree. The lack of public support manifests itself in lower college enrollment, reduced persistence to the degree, the retrenchment of government appropriations, and the decline in foundation and private philanthropy. By renewing and dramatically increasing its civic role in assisting and identifying sustainable solutions to the current economic, health, environmental, educational, and social challenges, colleges and universities will regain the public trust by becoming engaged institutions and positive social actors. At that time, a college degree will be valued as a public good and not just a private entitlement.

Higher education will need to attend to its traditional role of providing a compelling undergraduate education while expanding the nation's innovative capacity through the creation and dissemination of new and consequential knowledge. These are necessary but not sufficient conditions for higher education's role as a valued and supported domain within the American social landscape. Essential to its future, higher education must expand its role in addressing social and economic inequality and deepen its commitment to raising a generation of antiracist, civic-minded, and democratically educated leaders capable of imagining and developing an inclusive and stable democratic society. Higher education's commitment to civic engagement is a down payment on this critical national priority. This mission will require the development and expansion of university-neighborhood partnerships, which will serve as the incubator for educational opportunity, increased social capacity, and democratic citizenship.

Higher Education and Civil Society

To recapture its founding mission, higher education must play a primary role in the restoration of American democracy. At its best, democracy is a fragile arrangement of popular government combined with a culture of reciprocal and equitable relationships.[1] This social equation always is in flux and at risk. Democratic governments rely on democratic cultures. This is more true than it was at almost any time in American history. We are living in a particular moment marked by acute social discord and seemingly intractable political conflicts. The resurrection of nativist populism is leading to a significant distrust of democratic institutions and their basic intellectual foundations. Authority of all sorts is questioned for its legitimacy. Reason, science, and objectivity are too often ignored and replaced with self-affirming ideologies and nonrationalist fascinations. The prevailing paranoia apparent in a significant percentage of the nation threatens to fracture the democratic belief that strangers can come to govern themselves through the rule of law, the ballot box, and governmental institutions.

Democratic values, norms, folkways, and traditions provide the social glue that holds diverse societies and their governments together. In civil society, many of these are found in nongovernmental institutions, such as schools, churches, the arts, and the arenas of everyday gatherings, that shape our moral and cultural beliefs. For democratic governments to flourish, they need civil societies that nurture the fundamentals of freedom of speech, religion and assembly, and, just as importantly, literacy, education, critical thinking, and social responsibility. It is difficult to develop and sustain democratic governance without a democratic culture that values personal empathy, individual freedom, social reciprocity, and the rule of law. The subsequent public national narrative is predicated on equality of opportunity and the political freedoms of democratic practice.[2] These aspirations are not only evident in the founding documents of the American republic but they resonate in the profound leadership of more recent revolutionary and democratic leaders such as Nelson Mandela in South Africa and Vaclav Havel in the Czech Republic.[3] In short, democratic governments require more than procedural democratic practices of elections and legislative practice. They also require civil societies that prepare and encourage democratic values, which include individual freedoms tempered by the mutuality of public trust, social reciprocity, personal empathy, and social responsibility.

For nearly 250 years, the American democratic experiment has mixed both success and failure. The nation's history is framed by a positive narrative of liberty, equality, and aspirational freedom while stained by an intractable litany of racial, gender, and class subordination. The American dream is framed on hope of an inclusive and just social order. It assumes that the combination of engaged citizens and a constitutional federalist architecture provides a pathway in overcoming any contradictions. At present, we continue to encounter a nation beset by rising economic inequality, racial segregation, and de facto educational apartheid. The growing economic class gap is well documented but may be no better illustrated than by the following statistic from a recent study of the Economic Policy Institute. In 1965, the CEO/average worker compensation ratio was 20–1. In 1989, the ratio grew to 58–1, and in 2018, it ballooned to 278–1.[4] The racial divide is illustrated by the failure of American schools to become integrated. They are as segregated today as they were in 1954, when the U.S. Supreme Court declared that "separate but equal" was unconstitutional.

Democracies flounder in periods of growing inequality. They threaten to disassemble in the face of heightened demographic and economic change. Given the major ethnic and racial changes emerging in the United States, coupled with the technological revolution and its inherent educational divide, it is no wonder that historian Richard Hofstadter's observation of the "paranoid style in American politics" has returned.[5] The current political atmosphere is eroding American democratic institutions. Journalist Ezra Klein has amply demonstrated the elements of America's deep polarization. While he explores many of the factors I have mentioned, his argument reduces to the one reliable variable that best correlates with the resurgence of our deepening divide, namely, racial division and racism itself.[6]

While many institutions are critical for the revival of an American democratic culture and a vibrant civil society with equitable politics, what is the fundamental role for American higher education in restoring a functioning democracy and building a more just society?

Clearly colleges and universities were founded in part to prepare leaders and citizens to be knowledgeable, informed, and civically responsible. Just as important, higher education fashions a more educated and creative workforce in service of a market-based, dynamic economy. This has been the traditional rationalization for the civic role of colleges and universities as they have protected themselves from claims of partisanship and fears of political interference. They have clung to an institutional identity as predominantly politically benign builders of social and scientific assets. But will this distanced traditional role restore a democracy that is reeling from internal conflicts founded on ethnic and racial ignorance and growing economic inequality? I have argued in this book that this traditional role is not only inadequate but inappropriate for this particular historical moment. Toward this end, colleges and universities, their national associations, and the public sector have specific contributions to make in rebuilding American democracy.

The University as Engaged Citizen

First and foremost, higher education must partner with the K–12 schools in reintroducing the fundamentals of basic civics as part of their respective curriculums. In order for citizens to fully participate in democratic governance, they must have a clear and evidenced understanding of how their government operates, how laws are made and enforced, and how elections work. They need a firm knowledge of their rights and obligations as engaged citizens and the various legitimate forms of political participation. And, of course, civics must include the unvarnished history of American democracy, which includes a full disclosure of its ethnic, racial, gender, and class exclusions and the historical conflicts and political movements to remove them. This type of civics teaches the ideals and values of the American federal system as a structure of governance and as an aspirational pathway for political change and social justice. This is the first commitment that is necessary for restoring American democracy, which now is threatened by nativist, racist, and anti-intellectual ideologies and subcultures built on paranoia and reliance on civic ignorance.

The nation's schools and colleges are in dire need of a full-blown renewal of civic education, but as I have argued, civic learning must be gained through knowledge as well as civic practice, or what I have called the arts of democracy. Both of these components are required. One without the other results in an entirely inadequate civic education. Civic learning must be about the pursuit of liberty and equality. These are the written and espoused values and goals in the founding documents of American democracy and, as such, civics are about engaged and informed citizens as agents for their own political destiny.

Second, universities and colleges must act as agents for democracy. The traditional model of the university as a "noncitizen, political absentee" is not only obsolete but counterintuitive. The days of former University of California, Berkeley, Chancellor Clark Kerr's ideal of the university as a "city of intellect" are inadequate to meet this moment.[7] Universities require the freedom to pursue the creation and dissemination of knowledge. To realize that goal in its fullest requires a democratic society that honors not only popular governance and its attendant political freedoms but also a civic culture that celebrates open discourse, rationality, and evidenced argument as opposed to comfortable opinion. Ultimately, a comprehensive education needs to be available to all who seek it. At present, these values and practices are in danger and, as such, so is higher learning. In this historical moment, colleges and universities must be agents for the protection and expansion of American democracy. Without it, higher education's promise of free and open inquiry will disappear.

Third, higher education must be a forceful agent of change in reducing the social and economic inequality that is surely eroding American democracy by creating a caste system of citizens seemingly destined to live outside of the functioning political economy. This growing phenomenon is an anathema to a healthy democracy. The anchor model of university-neighborhood partnerships stands as the most vibrant and promising strategy for higher education's assistance in this effort. While colleges and universities have played a dramatic role in diversifying and expanding access to their campuses through generous institutional financial aid programs over the past thirty years, it is clear that this does not, in and of itself, offset the powerful impact of the growing inequality generated by the current macroeconomic system. Added to the commitments to campus diversity and access to higher education, the anchor partnership model provides the most useful pathway for higher education's role as an agent for both an engaged democracy and a more equitable, dynamic economy.

Much of the neighborhood success from anchor partnerships is traced to the university's expenditure of social, physical, and financial assets. Social capital is deployed through the contributions of students, faculty, and administrators in an array of initiatives involving tutoring and mentoring; programs in literacy, fluency, reading readiness, and math competency; direct health-care services; community-based research and teaching; participation in the fine and performing arts in establishing community voices and legacies; the dissemination of public history; direct assistance in economic and small business development; and a number of similar community-centered deployments. Physical capital is shared by opening up the campus facilities to neighborhood organizations in a variety of ways, such as providing meeting spaces for nonprofits and campus community dialogues. Finally, the university expends financial capital through hiring and purchasing polices that offer most-favored status to local vendors and residents.

While these are all elements of successful partnerships, the present moment is ripe for a national initiative that's more strategic in leveraging the work of the local university-neighborhood partnerships. This will require the assistance of the national higher education associations and the public sector.

The Need for Neighborhood Democracy

There is a genius to the federal model of American government, although distinct liabilities remain within this system of distributed authority and power. Any number of political theorists have celebrated the federal design. The most famous commentator is the nineteenth-century French diplomat

Alexis de Tocqueville, who famously visited the young American republic in the early 1830s. His formal mission was to review the new American penal system, but his real agenda was to help him gain a firm understanding of the American federal system and the essential political and social characteristics of this new democracy. The first part of his two-volume classic, *Democracy in America,* appeared in 1835 and the second in 1850. It is revered as a masterpiece of political science for its breadth and depth in uncovering the promise and pitfalls of the American experiment in governance.[8] He wanted to assess how this political design deeply valued liberty while supporting social equality, by which he meant the equality of opportunity.[9]

Having been witness to the ideals of the failed French Revolution and its descent into despotic violence, de Tocqueville was sobered that the pursuit of personal liberty without an accompanying system of rights, obligations, and laws would not temper the worst human instincts. In addition, he believed that the force of history was to create a true equal standing for all citizens while not crushing individual liberty. He was impressed by the American system of distributed power through the checks and balances in the federated layers of governance. Like Alexander Hamilton, he feared an unhealthy tyranny by an uninformed majority pursuing their own self-interest by crushing the rights of the minority. Through its diffused layers of authority, the federal model promised a greater probability of democratic stability, and hence it would keep the democratic experiment alive where other nations had failed.

There were two areas of particular concern for de Tocqueville. He observed the egoism and selfishness latent in a culture celebrating personal liberty at the cost of social community. He ultimately concluded that the remarkable and somewhat unique American pattern of forming voluntary and altruistic community associations would temper such individualistic sensibilities, particularly in the acquisition of money, wealth, and economic advantage. He ultimately concluded that this voluntaristic communitarian practice would allow the "habits of their hearts" to modify the impulse for unbridled individualism.[10] In other words, the ubiquitous presence of civic engagement could rescue democracy from its base instincts.

De Tocqueville was deeply troubled by the pervasive and insidious presence of slavery and how its obvious contradictions could inevitably destroy the nation. He identified slavery as a scourge embedded throughout American society and was prescient in fearing the inevitable disaster of the Civil War twenty-five years later. He had no clear sense of how and when the republic could free itself from this inherent contradiction.

But with all of that said, we are left with a federalist political structure that contains mechanisms for reform and significant change. The virtues of a multicentric arrangement allow citizens to seek opportunities and redress from sometimes competing levels of governmental agencies. This arrangement allows for local solutions when in concert with constitutional values and laws. But federalism has a history of discriminatory outcomes based on the suppression of minorities and unpopular policies, particularly at the local level. It has led to regional parochialisms that reinforce class, race, gender, and ethnic suppression. In and of itself the structure of federalism is no guarantee of equality, liberty, and justice. It requires a democratic culture that claims and protects these very values. A democratic civic culture is necessary for a robust, just, and dynamic democratic order, and the civil society is where values of community and reciprocity are taught and reinforced.

The present federalist system retains pathways for reform but consistently ignores or omits the voices and needs of poor Black and Brown neighborhoods. This is but another name for systems of bias such as institutionalized racism. The current arrangement of power and authority consistently ignores these communities when it comes to the distribution of opportunity and participation. One of the strategies in support of their needs, voices, and creativity is the anchor model of university partnerships. This approach begs a broader understanding of federalism.

A different layer of federalism—namely, neighborhood democracy—can be valued and supported in these new partnerships. My argument contends that the larger political implications of university anchor partnerships are important to recognize. The limits of contemporary federalism are empirical. The shadow neighborhoods are left out of any meaningful impact on national and local policy. Absent those rare moments of insurgency by the poor, Black, and Brown populations, the political parties are so dense with well-financed interest groups that they fail in adequately responding to the least economically positioned of their constituents. Similarly, local and city governments too often defer to the political influence of business interests, real estate groups, and some employee unions. The result is the displacement of their least politically and economically positioned communities. As the old saying goes, "If you are not at the table, you are on the menu."

University-neighborhood partnerships present a potential new arena for positive change. The anchor work provides some evidence that effective partnerships provide greater leadership capacity in shadow neighborhoods. The campuses can legitimize the previously silenced voices of their local communities and partners. There also is a solid literature for us to draw upon when envisioning the political implications of anchor partnerships and neighborhood engagement that could lead to a more robust democracy.

In the wake of President Lyndon Johnson's "war on poverty" legislation in the 1960s, Milton Kotler authored a prescient little book that chronicled the organization, impact, and political importance of that initiative in specific cities. *Neighborhood Government: The Local Foundations of Political Life* proved to be a brilliant critical review of community action programs (CAPs) funded by the Johnson legislation.[11] Designed as an antipoverty program that would circumvent what were longstanding urban political machines rife with local patronage and favoritism, the CAPs received direct federal funding. They were composed of local public neighborhood corporations created for the purpose of dispensing federal funds in support of a variety of antipoverty initiatives and economic programs advancing neighborhood employment, business creation, social welfare, and community development. In Kotler's account, these CAPs technically were not separate, new layers of government but public entities with spending authority for the implementation and leadership of the federal program.

One clear example identified by Kotler, the Bedford-Stuyvesant Community Corporation of that Brooklyn neighborhood, represented 300,000 residents who were largely absent from the political landscape of New York City's Democratic machine in the 1960s. The heavily African American neighborhood suffered from high levels of unemployment, extremely low income, and virtually no business development beyond small family businesses. The creation of this new entity would first create an active forum for neighborhood representative democracy and then a viable and financed political vehicle for significant economic and social neighborhood change. Similarly, Kotler chronicles the creation of the East Central Citizens Organization (ECCO) of Columbus, Ohio, in the same decade. It represented 6,500 local residents. All in all, the Johnson program created seventy CAPs around the nation.

Typically, the entities were organized by asking local residents to register as members of the corporation or community organization. From those healthy membership rolls, a governing council would be elected. From there, the usual organizing bodies would establish governing procedures for proper quorums, meetings, and decision-making authority. Kotler characterized this period as a moment of direct local democracy within neighborhoods without any manifest political influence and cast outside the existing power structures.

For a while, these new political entities were successful in directing federal funding to its intended destinations and programs. They circumvented the local political machines that were wedded to vested interests. That had proved to be a formula for maintaining the urban status. Unfortunately, the community action programs gradually lost influence as other political forces took precedence. The Vietnam War's impact on national priorities and the dramatic rise in mass protests crowded out these neighborhood programs.

With the change in presidential administration from Johnson to Richard Nixon, along with political opposition of mayors and governors, funding was reduced and eventually eclipsed. The programs ended and so did a moment of neighborhood democracy. For their advocates, the moment passed. Law and order became the framework for domestic politics. What looked so promising for local activism suddenly was eclipsed by larger forces. As I look back on this period, I recall John Lennon's famous line, "Life is what happens while you are busy making other plans."[12]

Kotler wanted these local public corporations to be included in city charters so that they would have standing as centers of expertise and resources.[13] To Kotler, this would ensure their long-term stability and impact. While the particular period and programs that he chronicled were largely pushed out, the concept has endured. Terry L. Cooper, professor emeritus of public policy at the University of Southern California, has outlined the adoption of the neighborhood government in Los Angeles with the advent of mandated "neighborhood councils" in the City Charter in the 1990s under the guidance of the Los Angeles Department of Neighborhood Empowerment. The approach proliferated early on, with more than seventy councils. The University of Southern California maintains an active specialized research unit, the Neighborhood Participation Project, which chronicles their activity and impact.

Movements for poor people's political efficacy always face the prospects of either political co-optation or political resistance, or both. But the essential point of Kotler's approach retains its importance. His book serves to reawaken the need for added political structures within shadow neighborhoods so that their voices are politically vibrant and impactful. How else will the coefficients of inequality change significantly? Kotler described a new approach, albeit dated to a different era, but quite attractive in the current environment. To quote Cooper, "Kotler argues that democracy must be built locally from the bottom up."[14]

I find this approach quite promising for the renewal of American democracy, particularly during a time prone to autocratic impulses. These political instincts are firmly in place in one of the two major political parties. While there is no legal status for neighborhood government as the fourth branch of federalism, it is a needed dimension for expanded participatory democracy. It institutionalizes the voices, values, and needs of these long-ignored, and too often suppressed, communities. These new neighborhood arrangements can be agencies for innovation in designing solutions to indigenous challenges. They draw on inherent assets of these locales and they empower residents to become engaged, important, and valued citizens. To me, this fourth dimension calls for the anchor model that is embedded in university-neighborhood partnerships, which awaken the political imagination for a more complete form of engaged democracy.

We see this larger vision emerging in the work of Bruce Katz and "the new localism."[15] He argues that the hyperpartisanship at the national level has resulted in policy stagnation. Cities have been required to find ways of solving local challenges in confronting ineffectual economic development, environmental threats, social exclusion, and growing inequality. Instead of relying on heavy national policy and programs emanating from the federal government, cities of all sizes and locations are creating cross-disciplinary networks in finding sustainable solutions. Katz describes the traditional vertical policy approach of reliance on the federal government for new ideas and approaches as inadequate because of suffocating partisan differences. The new localism provides horizontal coalitions that accumulate local assets drawn from interdisciplinary expertise, social capital, and innovative finance. To quote Katz and Jeremy Nowak, "Neither Bernie Sanders's view of the federal government as the realm of most solutions nor Donald Trump's notion of economic nationalism fits the new global or local reality."[16]

When combining the ideas of Kotler, Cooper, and Katz, we can begin to assemble an argument for a new type of citizen politics that flows out of neighborhood partnerships. It stands against the current political menu of governmental options. Across the global scene, national politics distributes authority within one of four models. Crony capitalism is the residue of what is left of neo-capitalism. The latter was the belief that markets are the motor force of innovation and they should be left free to pursue global comparative advantages. This was thought to optimize profits and increase wealth while most efficiently deploying economic resources. After thirty or so years, neo-capitalism has produced heightened economic inequalities and social disparities, and increased environmental challenges. Most importantly, neo-capitalism led a crony capitalism that results in the appropriation of regulatory, trade, and tax policy by economic and political elites working in tandem for their own financial gain and political power. This model operated globally and may be responsible for the right-wing populism that is circumventing much of Europe.

Klepto-capitalism is the hyper version of crony capitalism. This is the hijacking of the state apparatus by specific elites directly associated with ruling regimes. They completely misappropriate governmental spending, resources, and assets for personal financial gain of those elites directly wedded to the national leader. Among them, one could list Turkey, Russia, Mexico, and, of course, the notorious Trump administration and Trump's related business associates. *The Economist* maintains an index of nations rated for levels of crony capitalism.[17]

State socialism has a variety of forms, but its most curious model is found in China. It is a centralized state socialist system that employs elements of a market economy. Traditional state socialism with its centrally planned economies found in the previous Cold War Soviet bloc of nations is largely absent today. Finally, social democracy is the prevalent system of the European Western democracies. It has been engulfed in a pitched political assault from right-wing populist movements critical of its commitment to social inclusion and progressive immigration policies. Unfortunately, for all of its commitment to social equality, it remains subject to significant social and economic inequalities. It relies on centralized social services agencies and large bureaucratic governmental agencies. France would be a prime example.

All of these models fail the dramatic challenges facing a world beset by intensifying climate change, national levels of growing economic inequality, the intensification of cultural and religious conflicts, and the massive growth of displaced people and refugees. Indeed, the entire concept of the nation state is under interrogation by tribalist politics and unaccountable international actors, both empowered by an unfettered social media revolution. It is time for modern democracy to be reimagined as a more participatory system that combines citizen activism with inclusive, flexible, and innovative government. The introduction of neighborhood democracy may inspire all citizens to seek a greater role in government. If that awakening is accompanied by a democratic culture of empathy, reciprocity, and inclusion, it will be in large part due to American higher education's role in fulfilling its historic mission as agents for democracy.

In 2020, the United States was tested. It survived a direct attempt to abandon its electoral system by nullifying the popular vote in its presidential election to favor a sitting president who refused to accept his defeat. With more than fifty federal and state court challenges, the judicial arm of the federalist system held and American democracy survived its most significant domestic challenge since the Civil War. But this was a frail victory. Many in the Republican Party establishment sided with the president's attempt to overthrow the democratic order in favor of an autocrat. If nothing else, this sad episode demonstrates the vulnerability of democracy and the critical importance of defending it. Higher education must play a critical role in establishing a culture of democracy. As I have argued throughout this book, colleges and universities have an imperative to anchor democracy in the classroom, in democratic practice, and with those neighborhoods long ignored by the political mainstream.

This will require political cynicism and the absence of idealism to be replaced with a renewed belief in American democracy. This necessitates a new American dream to replace the former one that ignored the historical and enduring scars of racism and all forms of social subordination. Andrew Delbanco, Alexander Hamilton Professor of American Studies at Columbia University, has written about the death of the American dream in the face of the brutal realities of American history and predicted that a new one will emerge with a recognition of human decency and our individual rights and common obligations.[18] I contend that without an operative vision for the "good society," political movements for democratic expansion will never adequately grasp their positive impact. These movements surge during periods of crisis but too often fade in the face of implementing governmental reforms. In my teaching, I would instruct my own political science students that "if you don't envision the mountain top, you will never know how far you have climbed." Movements for change may be impactful, but absent a view of the ultimate goal and how to achieve it, activists will believe they have been ineffective because they don't have a clear vision of a good society and an inclusive democracy. At that point, the prospect of equitable social transformation stagnates.

Toward this end, higher education needs to build a new generation of democratic leaders and citizens capable of imagining and building that inclusive, equitable democracy and its accompanying dynamic economy. From my perspective, I believe they are more likely to come from the combination of a formidable and comprehensive education coupled with a deep engagement with the arts of democracy. University-neighborhood partnerships present our best hope in achieving this goal.

In these extraordinary times, the renewal of democracy will require exceptional leadership throughout higher education. Clearly, college and university presidents will play a critical role, but without significant faculty, student, and alumni allies, they likely will fall short. Campus leadership must come from the middle as well as the top. In addition, leadership succession is an imperative for the success of university-neighborhood partnerships. Presidents change, along with their institutional priorities, but so do leaders in schools, hospitals, nonprofit organizations, philanthropies, and local government leaders. It is important for all of those in and around universities to understand that power and influence resides in all parts of the organization. Leadership for partnerships is not the exclusive province of those at the top of the organization. When focused and resilient, faculty members and students hold remarkable potential for this positive work. So do community partners. Presidents respond to these civic stakeholders. In the end, if higher education is to protect, nurture, and develop democracy, it will be the responsibility of all its members. That is the charge for all of us dedicated to higher learning and its agents, the colleges and universities that have retained this obligation since they were founded.

Notes

1. See Steven Levitsky and Daniel Ziblatt, *How Democracies Die* (New York: Crown Publishing, 2018); see also Anne Applebaum, *Twilight of Democracy: The Seductive Lure of Authoritarianism* (New York: Doubleday, 2020).

2. For an interesting discourse on the American narrative, see Andrew Delbanco, *The Real American Dream: A Meditation on Hope* (Cambridge, MA: Harvard University Press, 1999).

3. See Nelson Mandela, *Conversations with Myself* (New York: Picador, 2011); Vaclav Havel, *Toward a Civil Society: Selected Speeches and Writing* (Prague: Lindove Noviny Publishing House, 1995).

4. Lawrence Mishel and Julia Wolfe, "CEO Compensation Has Grown 940% since 1978," Economic Policy Institute, Washington DC, August 14, 2019.

5. Richard Hofstadter, "The Paranoid Style in American Politics," *Harper's Magazine*, November 1964.

6. Ezra Klein, *Why We're Polarized* (New York: Avid Reader Press, 2020).

7. See Clark Kerr, *The Uses of the University* (Cambridge, MA: Harvard University Press, 1963), 198–229.

8. Alexis de Tocqueville, *Democracy in America*, Vol. 1 and 2, edited by J. P. Mayer (New York: Harper Collins, 1966).

9. Vincent Ostrom, *The Political Theory of the Compound Republic: Designing the American Experiment* (Lanham, MD: Rowman & Littlefield, 2008).

10. Alexis de Tocqueville, *Democracy in America*, Vol. 1 and 2, translated by Harvey Mansfield and Debra Winthrop (Chicago: University of Chicago Press, 2000), see Vol. 1, Part 2, Chapter 9, 275, 295; Vol. 2, Chapter 5, 491; and Vol. 2, Chapters 5, 8, & 11. For contemporary interpretations, see Robert Bellah, Robert Madden, William Sullivan, Ann Swidler, and Steven Tipton, *Habits of the Heart: Individualism and Commitment in American Life* (New York: Harper Collins, 1985); Parker Palmer, *Healing the Heart of Democracy: The Courage to Create a Politics Worthy of the Human Spirit* (San Francisco: Jossey-Bass, 2014); and John Horvat, "Where Are America's Habits of the Heart," *Crisis Magazine*, August 7, 2017.

11. Milton Kotler, *Neighborhood Government: The Local Foundations of Political Life* (Lanham, MD: Lexington Books, 1969).

12. A song lyric from "Beautiful Boy" by John Lennon, recorded on *Double Fantasy*, released November 17, 1980, Geffen Records.

13. See Terry L. Cooper's "Critical Introduction" in Milton Kotler, *Neighborhood Government: The Local Foundations of Political Life*, 2nd ed. (Lanham, MD: Lexington Books, 2003), xvii–xxxvii.

14. Terry L. Cooper, "Critical Introduction," xxxv.

15. Bruce Katz and Jeremy Nowak, *The New Localism: How Cities Can Thrive in an Age of Populism* (Washington DC: Brookings Press, 2017).

16. Katz and Nowak, *The New Localism*, 5.

17. See *The Economist*, "Our Crony-Capitalism Index: Planet Plutocrat," March 15, 2014.

18. Delbanco, *The Real American Dream*.

ABOUT THE AUTHOR

Richard Guarasci was the longest-serving president of Wagner College, becoming president emeritus on his retirement in 2019. He joined the college in 1997 as provost and vice president for academic affairs. He was previously dean of Hobart College at the Hobart and William Smith Colleges. Prior to that he served as a faculty member and dean at St. Lawrence University, Canton, New York.

He has served both as a member of the board of directors, and board chair of the Association of American Colleges & Universities, Campus Compact, the Coalition of Urban and Metropolitan Universities, the New American Colleges and Universities, New York State Higher Education Services Corporation, and Project Pericles. He has also served on the Civic Learning and Democratic Engagement National Task Force and the Anchor Institution Task Force.

INDEX

Made in the USA
Middletown, DE
16 July 2023

35287176R00110